SYSTEM CENTER 2012 R2 CONFIGURATION MANAGER

Automation from Zero to Hero

Raphael Perez

PUBLISHED BY

Raphael Perez (http://www.thedesktopteam.com/raphael/)

ISBN: 978-1508712909 (print)

Cover Image © Cleber Marques (contato@clebermarques.com)

Warning and Disclaimer

Feedback Information

We would like to hear from you. If you have any comments about how we could improve the quality of this book, please do not hesitate to contact us by sending an e-mail to raphael@rflsystems.co.uk

Foreword

Whenever I'm at a IT conference or talking with IT Pro's, PowerShell is always a hot topic of conversation. IT Professionals like you rely heavily on scripts and automation to accomplish more with less. Whether you consider PowerShell a trick of the trade or tool of the trade, Raphael shows you how to quickly master PowerShell automation for Configuration Manager. Even if you're new to PowerShell, his step by step examples get you on the fast track right from the start.

Raphael's real-world experience with Configuration Manager takes front stage as he provides many valuable examples such as managing your infrastructure, as optimizing your patch Tuesday routine, or pinpointing trouble with distributing applications and packages. I really like how Raphael takes you through a clear, purposeful journey to automation productivity.

Regardless of where you sit on the PowerShell knowledge curve, pull up a keyboard, open your PowerShell console, and enjoy your new-found hero status!

Dave Randall
Senior Program Manager
Microsoft Enterprise Client & Mobility

Dedicatory

I would like to dedicate this book to my wife Francielle and my daughter Lara; thanks for putting up with me and for your support and patience while I was writing this Book. Thank you Francielle and Lara, you will always be in my heart.

About the Author

Raphael Perez

Raphael Perez is an Enterprise Client Management MVP (http://bit.ly/14JclJl) based in the United Kingdom, he specialises in System Center Configuration Manager (including OS Deployment) and other System Center products (Operations Manager, Service Manager, etc.).

He is an IT professional with over fourteen years of experience and has been working with Microsoft Management Solutions since 2002. Raphael is talented in IT and can easily produce bulletproof solution at the drop of a hat. He is post-graduated in Computer Network and Telecommunications and Microsoft Certified Professional (MCP, MCSA Security, MCSE Security, MCTS, MCITP, and MCT).

He is a Community leader attending physical and virtual meetings and engaging with the community across several forums, twitter (http://twitter.com/dotraphael), LinkedIn (http://www.linkedin.com/in/dotraphael), his personal site (http://www.rflsystems.co.uk) and his personal blog (http://www.thedesktopteam.com/raphael/).

Raphael owns RFL Systems' (http://www.rflsystems.co.uk/), a System Center specialized consultancy and training services within the United Kingdom and has been working in a number of different System Center Configuration Manager and OS Deployment projects from small to enterprise environments across the UK.

About the Contributors and Reviewers

David Nudelman

David Nudelman is a Windows Expert – IT Pro MVP and is a blogger and speaker for TheDesktopTeam.Com. He focuses on Desktop Strategy, currently consulting on Desktop Transformation and Bring-your-own-device projects. David has always been secretly in love with Active Directory. He is known for his very informal style when delivering speeches at conferences. You can find out more about him on Twitter (https://twitter.com/nudelmanuk) or on his personal blog (http://www.thedesktopteam.com/david/).

Heinrich Pelser

Heinrich Pelser is an Enterprise Consultant born in South Africa but made Essex his home in 1999. He has been working with configuration Manager since 2007 and is a blogger and speaker for TheDesktopTeam.Com. Heinrich always speaks his mind and does not pull any punches. You can follow him on Twitter (https://twitter.com/Heinrich_Pelser) and his blogs about System Center and the Private Cloud bits at http://www.thedesktopteam.com/Heinrich/.

Panu Saukko

Panu Saukko, Enterprise Client Management MVP and MCT, is a consultant and trainer at ProTrainIT (http://www.protrainit.fi/) and is based in Finland. He has over 20 years' experience working with Microsoft technologies. Panu has worked with SMS and Configuration Manager beginning with SMS 1.2 and has created training courseware for multiple Microsoft products over the years. Panu has been a MVP since 2005.

Table of Contents

ist of Figures

List of Tables

Part I - Overview

For most Configuration Manager administrators, the Configuration Manager console is more than sufficient to perform the necessary operations. However, you are limited to what the console is designed to handle. For more complex tasks, or those that might extend beyond the scope of the console, you need an alternative. Today the best tool for this is PowerShell.

PowerShell is, without any doubt, the greatest scripting language available in the Microsoft world. It is easy to create a simple and a complex automation tasks and it can, by itself, automate anything. The integration with Configuration Manager is now allowing us, IT Pros, to create complex automation tasks in just few minutes and using only few lines of code, as opposite to hundreds when not using the Configuration Manager cmdlets.

With PowerShell, if you can work with one item, such as an application, package or collection, you can work with 10, 100 or 1000 with practically very little extra effort.

This book was created to allow you to learn how to use WMI and Configuration Manager PowerShell cmdlets to automate tasks and include a number of scripts for automating Configuration Manager tasks using PowerShell. Some of the scripts are one or two line commands. Others are scripts that are more complicated. You do not have to be a PowerShell expert to use the scripts, although certainly the greater your PowerShell experience is, the more you will be able to take from these scripts and customize them to meet your requirements.

This book has not been created to teach you about PowerShell nor Configuration Manager as you should have minimum knowledge of the following software and technologies, including but not limited to System Center Configuration Manager, PowerShell, WMI, Active Directory, SQL Server and Windows. Knowledge of any scripting language is beneficial.

This book has been organized in 7 parts. The first part gives an overview of the automation, where we talk about PowerShell, WMI, Tools and gives you enough information about the Configuration Manager PowerShell module and some tips that will help you when developing and troubleshooting Configuration Manager PowerShell scripts.

The second part, called Warming Up, is where we start to see the Configuration Manager PowerShell cmdlets and learn a bit about WMI and some of the benefits of using Configuration Manager PowerShell cmdlets and WMI together.

The 3rd part, called Assets and Compliance is where we look at scripts to manage Collections, Software Metering, etc.

The 4th part, called Software Library is where we look at scripts to manage Applications, Packages, Software Updates, Operating Systems, etc.

The 5th part, called Administration is where we will look at scripts to manage a Configuration Manager site and hierarchy.

The 6th part, called Console Extension is where we look at how to extend the Configuration Manager console.

The 7th and last part, called Extras is where we look at few other scripts, like Creating Folders, moving object into folders, etc.

During the reading of the book, you will be provided example of scripts and to help easy identification of codes and scripts, they are formatted like the following example, on grey background

```
$Process = Get-Process
$Process | select *
```

Note: All scripts used in this book can be downloaded from http://bit.ly/SCCM2012AutomationExamples.

Additional Resources

TheDesktopTeam.com (www.thedesktopteam.com)

TheDesktopTeam.com is a Desktop community in the United Kingdom specialized in desktop management, including but not limited to Active Directory, Configuration Manager, PowerShell, etc. and there you can find many scripts and tips on how to automate Configuration Manager with PowerShell.

I hope this is the first place you go to for additional Configuration Manager and PowerShell resources. As you might expect, my own blog is hosted on the TheDesktopTeam.com community website and includes great Configuration Manager content.

RFLSystems.co.uk (www.rflsystems.co.uk)

RFLSystems.co.uk is Raphael's personal site where he share a series free resources, including the most know being a Configuration Manager Health Check Toolkit that is available for 2007 and 2012 R2 versions of Configuration Manager.

PowerShell.com (www.powershell.com)

PowerShell.com is an educational and community site for PowerShell People. There you will find resources to help you learn and master PowerShell along with forums for communicating.

Dr. Tobias Weltner, creator of PowerShell.com, has also written one of most famous PowerShell books, called Mastering PowerShell, that is available for free at http://powershell.com/cs/blogs/ebookv2/default.aspx

What is PowerShell?

PowerShell, or Windows PowerShell, is a Windows command-line interface designed for system administrators to automate the administration of system resources by the execution of commands directly or through scripts.

Most shells, including Cmd.exe and UNIX shells, operate by executing a command or utility in a new process, and presenting the results to the user as text. Over the years, many text processing utilities have evolved to support this interaction. These shells also have commands that are built into the shell and run in the shell process. In most shells, because there are few built-in commands, many utilities have been created.

One example would be the `dir` command in Cmd.exe. This command would list files and folders in a specific folder.

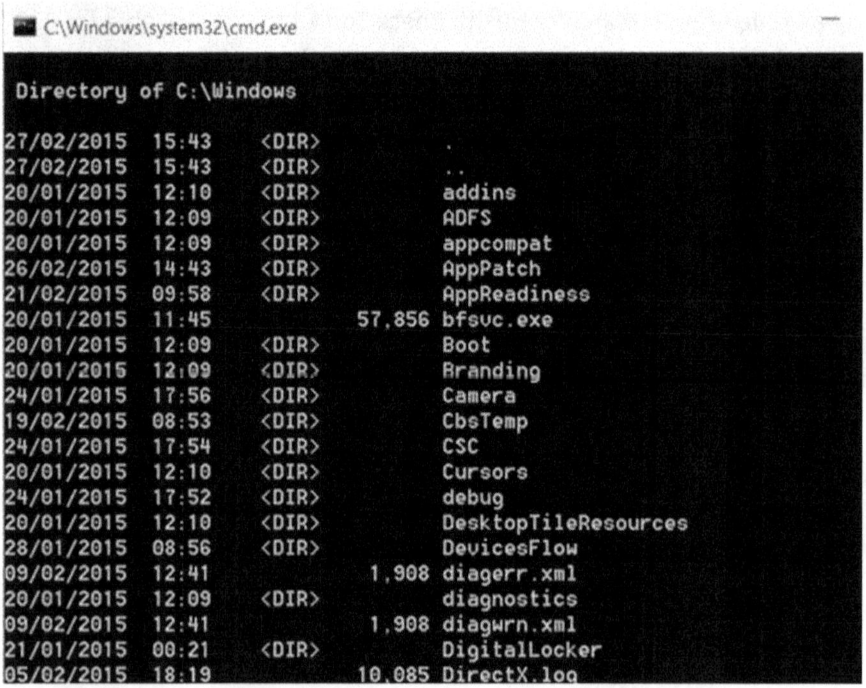

Figure 1. Part I – dir command in cmd.exe

In PowerShell, the command `dir` could also be used, however, it is only an alias for the `Get-ChildItem` cmdlet.

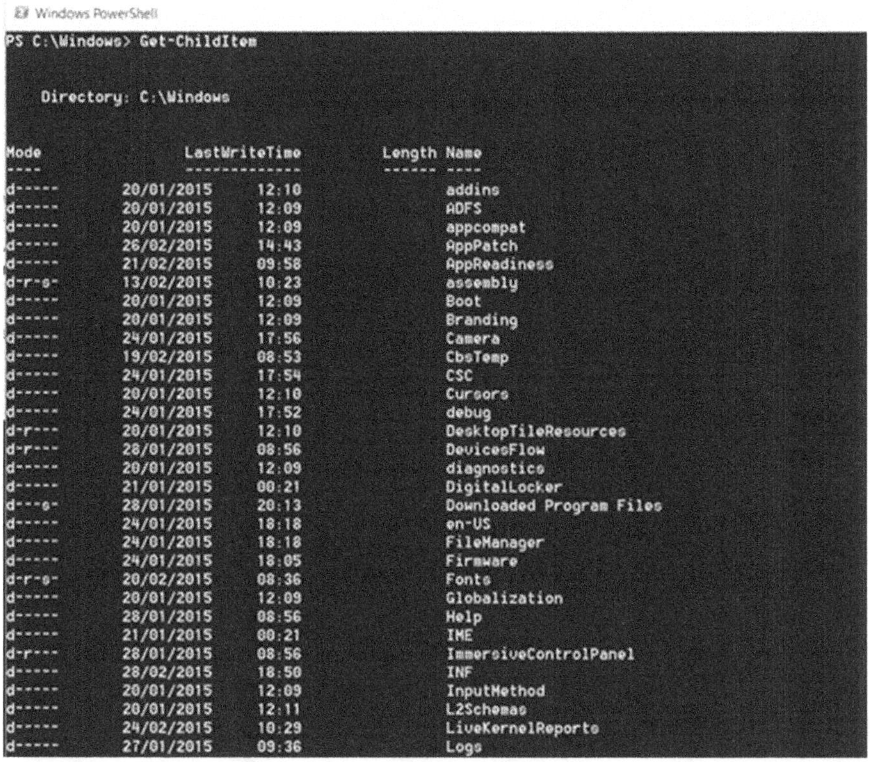

```
Windows PowerShell
PS C:\Windows> Get-ChildItem


    Directory: C:\Windows


Mode                LastWriteTime         Length Name
----                -------------         ------ ----
d-----       20/01/2015     12:10                addins
d-----       20/01/2015     12:09                ADFS
d-----       20/01/2015     12:09                appcompat
d-----       26/02/2015     14:43                AppPatch
d-----       21/02/2015     09:58                AppReadiness
d-r-s-       13/02/2015     10:23                assembly
d-----       20/01/2015     12:09                Boot
d-----       20/01/2015     12:09                Branding
d-----       24/01/2015     17:56                Camera
d-----       19/02/2015     08:53                CbsTemp
d-----       24/01/2015     17:54                CSC
d-----       20/01/2015     12:10                Cursors
d-----       24/01/2015     17:52                debug
d-r---       20/01/2015     12:10                DesktopTileResources
d-r---       28/01/2015     08:56                DevicesFlow
d-----       20/01/2015     12:09                diagnostics
d-----       21/01/2015     00:21                DigitalLocker
d---s-       28/01/2015     20:13                Downloaded Program Files
d-----       24/01/2015     18:18                en-US
d-----       24/01/2015     18:18                FileManager
d-----       24/01/2015     18:05                Firmware
d-r-s-       20/02/2015     08:36                Fonts
d-----       20/01/2015     12:09                Globalization
d-----       28/01/2015     08:56                Help
d-----       21/01/2015     00:21                IME
d-r---       28/01/2015     08:56                ImmersiveControlPanel
d-----       28/02/2015     18:50                INF
d-----       20/01/2015     12:09                InputMethod
d-----       20/01/2015     12:11                L2Schemas
d-----       24/02/2015     10:29                LiveKernelReports
d-----       27/01/2015     09:36                Logs
```

Figure 2. Part I – Get-ChildItem cmdlets in PowerShell

Unlike most shells, PowerShell is built on top of the .NET Framework common language runtime (CLR) and the .NET Framework, and accepts and returns .NET Framework objects. PowerShell provides full access to the Component Object Model (COM) and Windows Management Instrumentation (WMI), enabling administrators to perform administrative tasks on both local and remote Windows systems as well as WS-Management and Common Information Model (CIM) enabling management of remote Linux systems and network devices. This fundamental change in the environment brings entirely new tools and methods to the management and configuration of Windows.

The main differences between PowerShell and other shells are:

- PowerShell does not process text. Instead, it processes objects based on the .NET Framework platform.
- PowerShell comes with a large set of built-in commands with a consistent interface.
- All shell commands use the same command parser, instead of different parsers for each tool. This makes it much easier to learn how to use each command.

In PowerShell, administrative tasks are generally performed by cmdlets (pronounced command-lets), which are specialized .NET classes implementing a particular operation. Sets of cmdlets may be combined into scripts, executables (which are standalone applications), or by instantiating regular .NET classes (or WMI/COM Objects). These work by accessing data in different data stores, like the file system or registry, which are made available to the PowerShell runtime via PowerShell providers.

PowerShell also provides a hosting API with which the PowerShell runtime can be embedded inside other applications. These applications can then use PowerShell functionality to implement certain operations, including those exposed via the graphical interface. This capability has been used by Microsoft Exchange Server since version 2007, to expose its management functionality as PowerShell cmdlets and providers and implement the graphical management tools as PowerShell hosts which invoke the necessary cmdlets. Other Microsoft applications including Microsoft SQL Server, System Center Virtual Machine Manager, etc. also expose their management interface via PowerShell cmdlets.

Cmdlets

Cmdlets are internal PowerShell commands that enable you to perform an action and typically return a Microsoft .NET Framework object.

Cmdlets differ from commands in other command-shell environments in the following ways:

- Cmdlets are instances of .NET Framework classes; they are not stand-alone executables.
- Cmdlets can be created from as few as a dozen lines of code.
- Cmdlets do not generally do their own parsing, error presentation, or output formatting. Parsing, error presentation, and output formatting are handled by the PowerShell runtime.
- Cmdlets process input objects from the pipeline rather than from streams of text, and cmdlets typically deliver objects as output to the pipeline.
- Cmdlets are record-oriented because they process a single object at a time.

Parameters

Cmdlets parameters provide the mechanism that allows a cmdlet to accept input. Parameters can accept input directly from the command line, or from objects passed to the cmdlet through the pipeline, the arguments (also known as values) of these parameters can specify the input that the cmdlet accepts, how the cmdlet should perform its actions, and the data that the cmdlet returns to the pipeline.

Not every cmdlets accept parameter and when accepting, these parameters can be optional or required. When the cmdlets accept parameters, the parameter add information so the cmdlets know what to do.

There are two types of parameters: Named Parameters and Switch parameters. The Named parameters is a key-value pair, it means that each parameter requires a value, while the switch parameter is a Boolean parameter, it means, if the parameter is used, it normally represent a true value.

Variables

Variables store single information temporarily, so you can save some information to be used later on.

PowerShell differ from other development languages because you do not need to declare a variable, it creates new variables automatically when needed. Variables in PowerShell always start with a prefix "$".

To create a variable, you can use:

```
$variable = "Some value"
```

Arrays

Array is a variable. However, instead of storing single information, it stores multiple information temporarily.

PowerShell is clever and will "convert" a variable to an array when a command result multiple results.

To identify if a variable is an array or not, you can use:

```
$variable -is [Array]
```

It will return a Boolean value (true or false). If the result is an array, you can find the number of elements stored on it, using the property count that returns a numeric value:

```
$variable.Count
```

Pipeline

Pipelining (|) is used in PowerShell to join two statements so that the output of the first one, becomes the input of the second one, creating a chain of instructions.

As example, you can use the `Get-Process` cmdlets, that returns all running process in the computer, using the pipeline, you could filter it using the `Where-Object` cmdlets to return only a subset of the process. This can be achieved by running the following command:

```
Get-Process | Where-Object {$_.ProcessName -eq "Outlook" }
```

Objects

Objects are just a representation of something and PowerShell only works with objects. Everything that is typed into the PowerShell console is converted to object. Objects are composed by Properties and Methods:

- Properties: it is a variable for the object
- Methods: the object executes an action.

If you translate objects to the real life, an object would be a Person and the Properties would be Hair Size, Hair Colour, Number of Fingers, etc. while the Methods would be Run, Walk, Sleep, etc.

Similar to array, an object can be stored in a variable and to identify the object type, you can use:

```
$variable.GetType().FullName
```

It will return a string value.

Comparison Operators

You may often want to compare values and find values that match specified patterns. In PowerShell, this can be done via the comparison operators.

By default, all comparison operators are case-insensitive, it means that it does not make a difference between lower case and upper case characters. The table below represent a list of all case-insensitive operators:

Comparison Operator	Description
eq	Equal to
ne	Not equal to
gt	Greater-than
ge	Greater-than or equal to
lt	Less-than
le	Less-than or equal to
like	Match using the wildcard character (*)
notlike	Does not match using the wildcard character (*)
match	Matches a string using regular expressions
notmatch	Does not match a string using regular expressions
contains	Tells whether a collection or array of reference values includes a single test value
notcontains	Tells whether a collection or array of reference values does not includes a single test value
in	Tells whether a test value appears in a collection or array of reference values.
notin	Tells whether a test value does not appears in a collection or array of reference values.
replace	Changes the specified elements of a value

Table 1. Part I – PowerShell Comparison Operators

To make a comparison operator case-sensitive, precede the operator name with a "c" (i.e. the case-sensitive version of "-eq" is "-ceq"). To make the case-insensitivity explicit, precede the operator with an "i" (i.e. the explicitly case-insensitive version of "-eq" is "-ieq").

To validate if a string is equal to another string (case-insensitive), use the "eq" operator as per below example:

```
"abcd" -eq "ABCD"
```

This would return TRUE, and if you want to validate the case-sensitivity, that would return FALSE, you would use "ceq" operator as per below example

```
"abcd" -ceq "ABCD"
```

Functions

PowerShell has a series of internal commands. However, there are moments where the existing commands are not sufficient to perform actions needed. Functions are new commands, created by the user (or script) to perform some custom actions. They have three benefits:

- Shorthand: very simple shorthand for commands and immediately give the commands arguments to take along
- Combining: functions can make your work easier by combining several steps
- Encapsulating and extending: small but highly complex programs

The structure of the function is the same for all three instances, the only change is what the function does and how it does.

Scripts

PowerShell scripts are like batch files in the traditional cmd.exe console: scripts are text files that can include any PowerShell code. The file extension is typically PS1.

If you run a PowerShell script, PowerShell will read the instructions in it, and then execute them. As a result, scripts are ideal for complex automation tasks.

Script security

PowerShell makes certain requirements mandatory for their execution because scripts can contain potentially dangerous statements. Depending on the security setting and storage location, scripts must have a digital signature or be specified with their absolute or relative path names.

There are several execution policy restrictions for script from the most restrictive (Restricted) to the less restrictive (Unrestricted). To see what the current settings, execute the command Get-ExecutionPolicy and to change the PowerShell security, an administrator can execute the command Set-ExecutionPolicy. The change is permanent and the security will be applied every time a script runs.

Executing Scripts

When you have the script created, you have two options to invoke a script. Via the PowerShell console, executing:

```
.\Script.ps1
```

Or external to the PowerShell console, invoking it via the PowerShell.exe command line, as per bellow example:

```
powershell.exe -NoExit -Command "& '.\Script.ps1'"
```

It is also possible to override the PowerShell security during the execution of a script when it is invoked via PowerShell.exe. This can be achieved using the parameter ExecutionPolicy as per the example bellow:

```
powershell.exe -executionPolicy bypass -NoExit -File
"c:\temp\Script.ps1"
```

Windows Management Instrumentation (WMI)

For many years, Configuration Manager only used the Windows Management Instrumentation (WMI) to perform the required tasks. Configuration Manager Console was only an interface for the WMI for listing results and perform calls for WMI methods to make changes. So, one of the most important technologies that Configuration Manager utilizes internally is WMI and most, if not all, Configuration Manager operations can be done with WMI.

With the introduction of PowerShell on top of Configuration Manager, you would imagine that using WMI would not be necessary anymore. However, it is not true. As the PowerShell module for Configuration Manager is relatively new, Microsoft did not re-write the Configuration Manager code. Instead, they added a new PowerShell module on top of the underlying WMI layer as a new interface for the Configuration Manager administrator.

In essence, the Configuration Manager PowerShell module allows an easy integration with the WMI. Because the PowerShell support in Configuration Manager is under constant development and not complete, knowing WMI is still required for many of the automation tasks.

WMI is a set of specifications from Microsoft for extensions to the Windows Driver Model (WDM) that provides an operating system interface through which instrumented components provide information and notification.

WMI was created for consolidating the management of devices and applications in a network and is a Microsoft's implementation of the Web-Based Enterprise Management (WBEM) and Common Information Model (CIM) standards from the Distributed Management Task Force (DMTF).

WMI allows scripting languages like VBScript or PowerShell to manage Microsoft Windows computers, both locally and remotely and is preinstalled in Windows 2000 and newer OSs.

The purpose of WMI is to define a proprietary set of environment-independent specifications, which allow management information to be shared between management applications. WMI prescribes enterprise management standards and related technologies for Windows that work with existing management standards, such as Desktop Management Interface (DMI) and Simple Network Management Protocol (SNMP). WMI complements these other standards by providing a uniform model. This model represents the managed environment through which management data from any source can be accessed in a common way.

WMI Architecture

The following diagram shows the relationship between the WMI infrastructure and the WMI providers and managed objects, and it also shows the relationship between the WMI infrastructure and the WMI consumers.

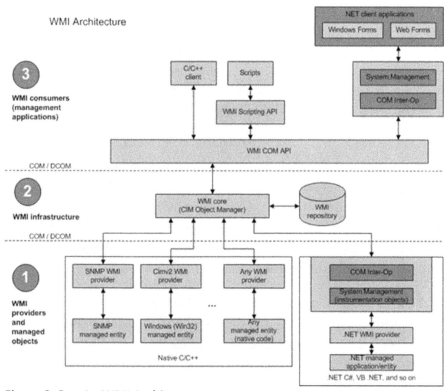

Figure 3. Part I – WMI Architecture

Source: http://msdn.microsoft.com/en-us/library/aa394553(v=vs.85).aspx

WMI Components

Managed objects and WMI providers

A WMI provider is a COM object that monitors one or more managed objects for WMI. A managed object is a logical or physical enterprise component, such as a hard disk drive, network adapter, database system, operating system, process or service.

Similar to a driver, a provider supplies WMI with data from a managed object and handles messages from WMI to the managed object. WMI providers consist of a DLL file and a Managed Object Format (MOF) file that defines the classes for which the provider returns data and performs operations. Providers, like WMI C++ applications, use the Component Object Model (COM) API for WMI

An example of a provider is the preinstalled Registry provider, which accesses data in the system registry. The Registry provider has one WMI class, StdRegProv, with many methods but no properties. Other preinstalled providers, such as the Win32 provider, usually have classes with many properties but few methods, such as Win32_Process or Win32_LogicalDisk. The Registry provider DLL file, Stdprov.dll, contains the code that dynamically returns data when requested by client scripts or applications.

WMI MOF and DLL files are located in %WINDIR%\System32\Wbem, along with the WMI Command-Line Tools, such as Winmgmt.exe and Mofcomp.exe. Provider classes, such as Win32_LogicalDisk, are defined in MOF files, and then compiled into the WMI repository at system start up.

WMI infrastructure

The WMI infrastructure is a Microsoft Windows operating system component. The WMI infrastructure has two components: the WMI service (winmgmt), including the WMI Core, and the WMI repository.

The WMI repository has multiple namespaces. The WMI service creates some namespaces such as root\default, root\cimv2, and root\subscription at system start up and preinstalls a default set of class definitions, including the Win32 Classes, the WMI System Classes, and others. The remaining namespaces found on your system are created by providers for other parts of the operating system or products.

 The WMI service acts as an intermediary between the providers, management applications, and the WMI repository. Only static data about objects is stored in the repository, such as the classes defined by providers. WMI obtains most data dynamically from the provider when a client requests it. You also can set up subscriptions to receive event notifications from a provider.

WMI consumers

A WMI consumer is a management application or script that interacts with the WMI infrastructure. A management application can query, enumerate data, run provider methods, or subscribe to events by calling either the COM API for WMI or the Scripting API for WMI. The only data or actions available for a managed object, such as a disk drive or a service, are those that a provider supplies.

Managed Object Format (MOF)

Managed Object Format (MOF) is the language used to describe Common Information Model (CIM) classes.

The recommended way for WMI providers to implement new WMI classes is in MOF files, which are compiled using `Mofcomp.exe` into the WMI repository. It is also possible to create and manipulate CIM classes and instances using the COM API for WMI.

A WMI provider normally consists of a MOF file, which defines the data and event classes for which the provider returns data, and a DLL file, which contains the code that supplies data.

Tools

System Center 2012 R2 Configuration Manager SDK

The Configuration Manager SDK provides information applicable to administrators who want to automate Configuration Manager through script and to developers adding features and extensions to base Configuration Manager functionality.

It contains documentation and samples that are useful in developing applications that access and modify Configuration Manager data and also provides comprehensive reference material for each Configuration Manager feature.

Figure 4. Part I – Configuration Manager 2012 R2 SDK

Download at http://www.microsoft.com/en-gb/download/details.aspx?id=29559

Online version at http://msdn.microsoft.com/en-us/library/hh948960.aspx

CMTrace

It is one of the most important tools for any Configuration Manager Administrator. With CMTrace, you are able to read in real time, Configuration Manager Logs.

Unlike its predecessor, cmtrace.exe is built-in in Configuration Manager, there is no need to download separate toolkits for it and can be found on the Configuration Manager site server, under <Installation Folder>\Tools.

Figure 5. Part I – CM Trace

WBEMTest.exe

WBEMTest.exe is included on every computer that has WMI installed. You can use it to quickly explore or confirm WMI details. However, WBEMTest.exe is only designed to be a support tool and does not have a friendly interface for browsing classes or instances compared to other tools available in the internet.

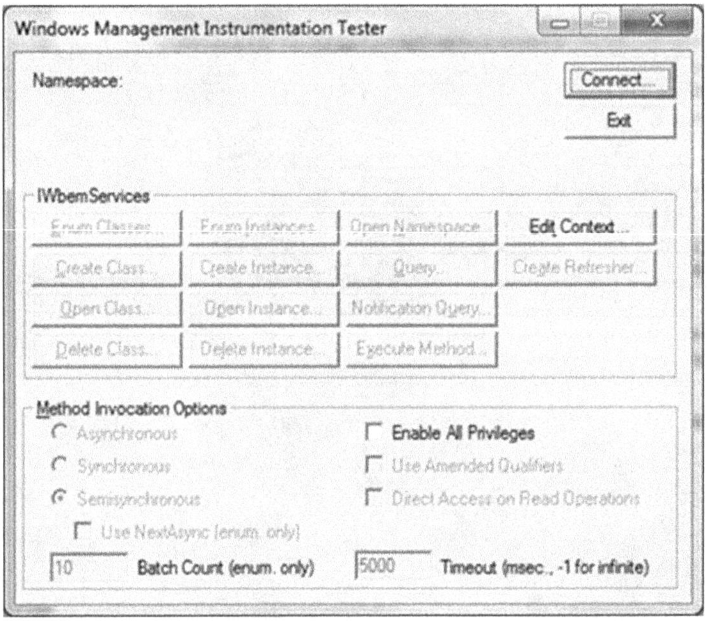

Figure 6. Part I – WBEMTest.exe

CIM Studio

Part of the WMI Administrative Tools that include: WMI CIM Studio: view and edit classes, properties, qualifiers, and instances in a CIM repository; run selected methods; generate and compile MOF files. WMI Object Browser: view objects, edit property values and qualifiers, and run methods.

Figure 7. Part I – CIM Studio

Download at http://www.microsoft.com/en-us/download/details.aspx?id=24045

WMI Explorer

There are many WMI Explorers out there that allows you to:

- Explore the full set of WMI management classes, objects and their properties
- Browse through objects and settings on remote machines
- Execute any WQL query and view the result set

The author's recommendation is the WMI Explorer from KS-Soft that can be downloaded at http://www.ks-soft.net/hostmon.eng/wmi/

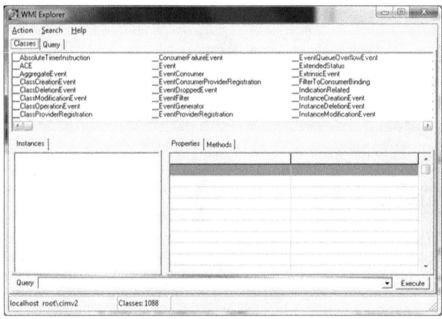

Figure 8. Part I – WMI Explorer

PowerShell ISE

The PowerShell Integrated Scripting Environment (ISE) is a host application for PowerShell. In PowerShell ISE, you can run commands and write, test, and debug scripts in a single Windows-based graphic user interface with multiline editing, tab completion, syntax colouring, selective execution, context-sensitive help, and support for right-to-left languages. You can use menu items and keyboard shortcuts to perform many of the same tasks that you would perform in the PowerShell console. For example, when you debug a script in the PowerShell ISE, to set a line breakpoint in a script, right-click the line of code, and then click Toggle Breakpoint.

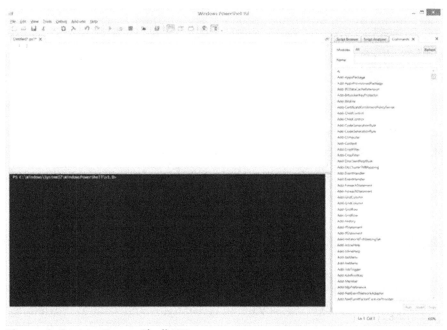

Figure 9. Part I – PowerShell ISE

Configuration Manager 2012 and PowerShell

For many years, scripting and automating tasks in a Configuration Manager environment was a tough task that could, easily, take days and weeks to be completed. This is because before Configuration Manager 2012 SP1 all automation is based on WMI. Additionally, the available documentation at the time was not designed for someone with little or no development experience.

With the release of Configuration Manager 2012 SP1, Microsoft finally introduced native PowerShell support. With the new Configuration Manager PowerShell cmdlets, Configuration Manager administrator (with basic knowledge of PowerShell) can automate tasks in minutes.

With over 500 PowerShell cmdlets, Configuration Manager 2012 allows a Configuration Manager administrator to perform most (if not all) functions from the PowerShell environment instead of using the admin console.

It is important to remember that PowerShell support is updated frequently. Also, if you want to use PowerShell with Configuration Manager, you should use the latest Configuration Manager Cumulative Update available as they contain bug fixes, enhanced cmdlets and, sometimes, new PowerShell cmdlets.

Connecting to the Configuration Manager PowerShell Environment

First, you need to make sure that PowerShell 3.0 or newer is installed on your system. If not, you can download it from http://www.microsoft.com/en-us/download/detalls.aspx?ld=34595. PowerShell 3.0 or newer is included in Windows Server 2012, Windows 8, and later Windows versions by default. Like many applications, PowerShell comes in a 32-bit version and a 64-bit version and the Configuration Manager 2012 SP1 PowerShell Module needs the 32-bit version.

Note: For Configuration Manager 2012 R2, the PowerShell module was re-written and it allows you to run on a 64-bit PowerShell, however, there are still cmdlets that only run on a 32-bit version of PowerShell.

Once you have the PowerShell 3.0 installed, you need to load the Configuration Manager 2012 module. You can achieve this in two different ways: using `import-module` or via Configuration Manager console.

In both ways, the Configuration Manager PowerShell module is referenced by the `ConfigurationManager.psd1` file that resides in the Configuration Manager install directory under the <Admin Console Installation Dir>\bin folder (i.e. D:\Configuration Manager\AdminConsole\bin\ConfigurationManager.psd1).

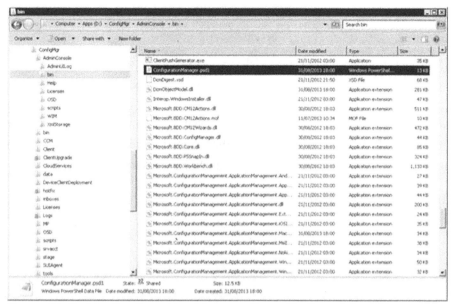

Figure 10. Part I – Configuration Manager PowerShell module path

Use the `import-module` command, when a PowerShell session is already open. From the command line you simply run the following command to load the module:

```
import-module D:\Configuration
Manager\AdminConsole\bin\ConfigurationManager.psd1
```

Figure 11. Part I – Importing Configuration Manager PowerShell module

After a few seconds the module will load and you will have access to all the Configuration Manager cmdlets. Keep in mind though that this only loads it for that session, so if you want to have it load any time you launch PowerShell you can add it to your PowerShell profile (http://technet.microsoft.com/en-us/library/ff461033.aspx).

Note: On Configuration Manager 2012 SP1, the PowerShell Module is a x86 (32-bit) version, it means that you need to open it on a 32-bit version of PowerShell. If you try to open on a 64-bits version, you will see the following error:

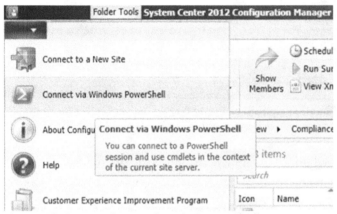

Figure 12. Part I – Importing Configuration Manager PowerShell module failure

Another way is loading PowerShell from the Configuration Manager Console. To do this, start by launching the Configuration Manager console. In the upper left corner, there is a blue rectangle. Click the white arrow in the blue rectangle, and choose "Connect via PowerShell".

Figure 13. Part I – Connecting via PowerShell

It will take a moment to load. Once it is loaded, you will see a prompt that contains your site code.

Figure 14. Part I – PowerShell via Configuration Manager console

Behind the Scenes and monitoring what is happening

Every time you use the console or the Configuration Manager PowerShell module, Configuration Manager uses WMI. Basically, it will record all activities on a log called smsprov.log on the server under <Installation Folder>\Logs

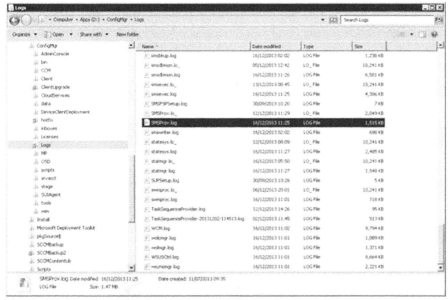

Figure 15. Part I – Behind the Scenes SMSProv.Log location

Once you open it (preferable using CMTrace), keep your attention to the lines that contains the following text:

- GetObjectAsync
- Requested class
- ExecQueryAsync
- Execute WQL

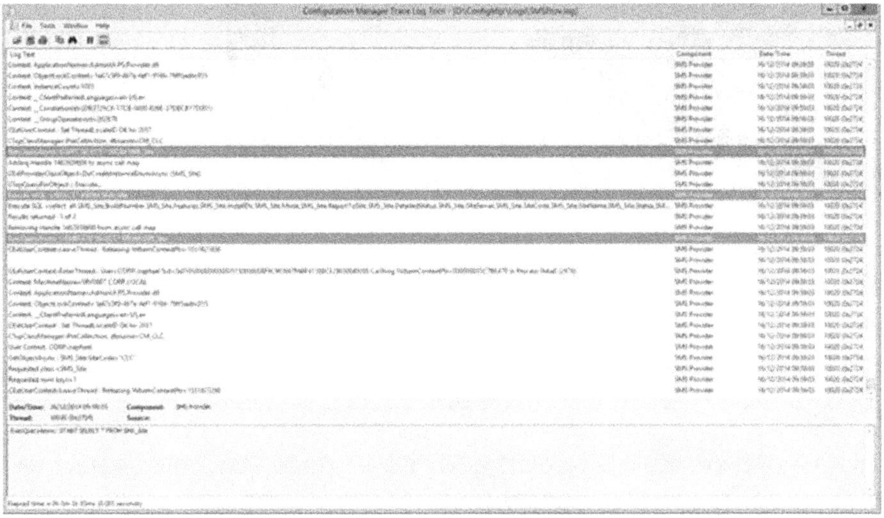

Figure 16. Part I – Behind the Scenes CMTrace with SMSProv.log

You may need to change the log level / log size of the provider. For tests and lab purposes, the author recommends using verbose for log level and the log size for at least 10MB.

To do this, navigate to the registry key HKEY_LOCAL_MACHINE \ Software \ Microsoft \ SMS \ Providers and set the following values:

- Logging Level = 0 (REG_DWORD)
- SQL Cache Logging Level = 1 (REG_DWORD)
- Log Size MB = 10 (REG_DWORD)

Cmdlets

Once you have the module loaded, simply type Get-Command -module ConfigurationManager to get a list of all the available cmdlets:

Figure 17. Part I – List of cmdlets

In addition, an easy way to see how many cmdlets you have, use the Count property as per following command:

```
(Get-Command -module ConfigurationManager).Count
```

On a SP1 CU3 environment, there are 511 cmdlets, 562 on a R2, up to CU3, environment and 597 on a R2 CU4 environment, as you can see below:

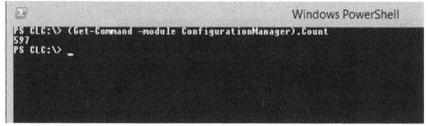

Figure 18. Part I – Count of cmdlets on R2 CU4 environment

Getting Help

To get information on the syntax of the cmdlets, simply type `Get-Help` and the name of the cmdlet

```
get-help Get-CMApplication
```

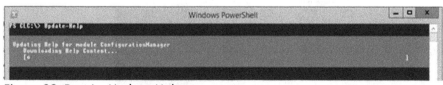

Figure 19. Part I – Get-help

Unfortunately, the version of the help installed is not current. To update the offline version, you can use the `update-help` cmdlet, that will connect to the internet and download the most up to date version of all PowerShell modules:

```
update-help
```

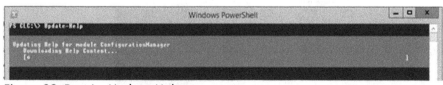

Figure 20. Part I – Update-Help

Or, if you are only interested in updating the ConfigMgr module only, use:

```
update-help -module configurationmanager
```

Figure 21. Part I – Update Configuration Manager help module

However, using the `update-help` may not be the fastest approach, as it will download all necessary updates from the internet. You can use the parameter `-online` that will open the browser with the most up to date version of the help.

```
get-help get-cmapplication -online
```

Figure 22. Part I – Get-help -online

Invalid Command

Now that you have the most up-to date help, let's start using the PowerShell, with the `Get-CMSite` cmdlet. Open the PowerShell, import the Configuration Manager module and type:

```
get-cmsite
```

Figure 23. Part I – Invalid Command

As you may see, PowerShell does not seem to understand this and you will get "This command cannot be run from the current drive. To run this command you must first connect to a Configuration Manager drive". This is because you may be pointing to the hard drive and not the Configuration Manager Site.

To do this, you can use the CD command to change to your site, so the command would be CD <SITE CODE>:

```
cd CLC:
```

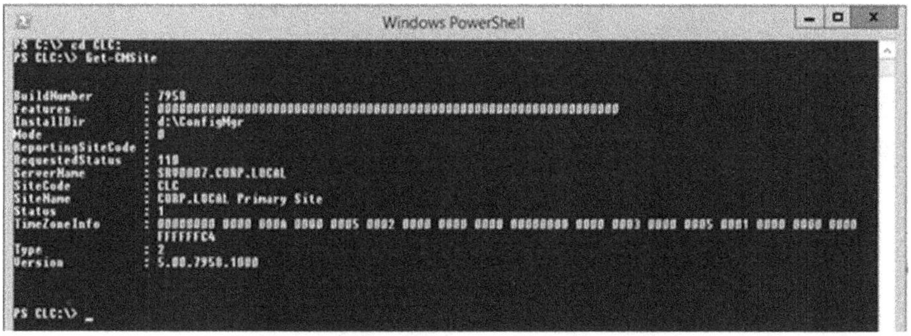

Figure 24. Part I – Change Directory Command

If you do not know the Site Code, you could use the get-psdrive to show all mapped drivers or to get only the Configuration Manager mapped drive (Configuration Manager Site), type:

```
get-psdrive -PSProvider CMSite
```

Figure 25. Part I – Get-PSDrive for CMSite provider

One easy solution to change the drive to the Configuration Manager drive would be using:

```
cd "$((Get-PSDrive -PSProvider CMSite).Name):"
```

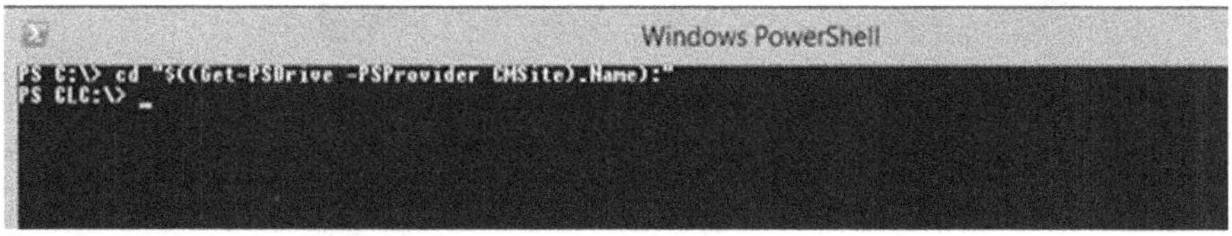

Figure 26. Part I – Automation mapped drive

Which Cmdlet?

Because there are many cmdlets, it is difficult to find the right one. The easiest way is to use the get-command cmdlet.

```
get-command
```

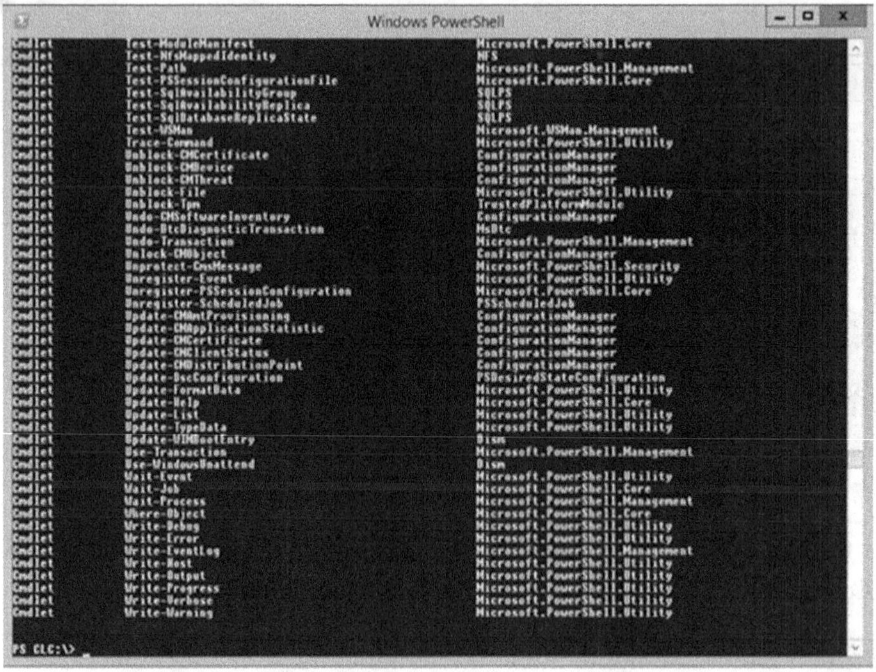

Figure 27. Part I – List of cmdlets

However, it will bring every single command available to you. If you would like to see only Cmdlets from the Configuration Manager module where the name has deplopymenttype, use:

```
get-command -Module ConfigurationManager -name *deploymenttype*
```

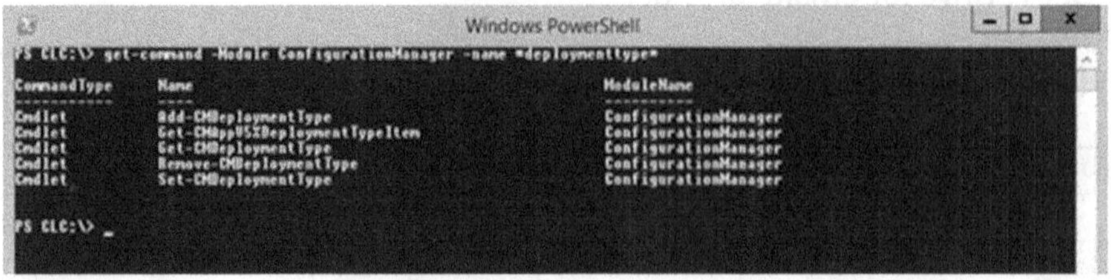

Figure 28. Part I – List of DeploymentType cmdlets

What is the command line?

Depending on the cmdlet used, might be variations of the command, where some parameters would be required in certain circumstances. For example, Add-CMDeploymentType requires different parameters when creating a MSI deployment type or when creating a Windows Store deployment type. In this scenario, the best solution is to use the show-command cmdlet

```
Show-command Add-CMDeploymentType
```

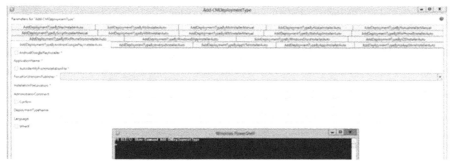

Figure 29. Part I – Show-command

Script running as a service account

Configuration Manager PowerShell modules are digitally signed and only users with the correct certificate installed in the Trusted Publishers are able to run Configuration Manager PowerShell cmdlets.

The certificate is installed the first time the user runs the Configuration Manager PowerShell when it is open via the Configuration Manager Console.

Figure 30. Part I – Script running as a service account (1)

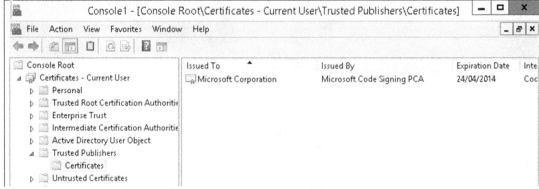

Figure 31. Part I – Script running as a service account (2)

Users without the certificate, after importing the Configuration Manager PowerShell module, would get "A drive with name 'xxx' does not exist" error message when trying to access the Configuration Manager PowerShell drive.

Figure 32. Part I – Script running as a service account (2)

The solution would be to install the certificate manually by accessing the ConfigurationManager.psd1 file properties.

Figure 33. Part I – Script running as a service account (3)

Unfortunately this is not always possible when dealing with service accounts. To overcome this issue, you can use the following PowerShell lines at the beginning of your script. In essence, these lines will get the certificate thumbprint from the ConfigurationManager.psd1 file and check if it exists in the Trusted Publisher for the users and if it does not, it will then install.

```
$ModulePath =
$env:SMS_ADMIN_UI_PATH.Replace("bin\i386","bin\ConfigurationManager.p
sd1")
$Certificate = Get-AuthenticodeSignature -FilePath "$ModulePath" -
ErrorAction SilentlyContinue
$CertStore = New-Object
System.Security.Cryptography.X509Certificates.X509Store("TrustedPubli
sher")
$CertStore.Open([System.Security.Cryptography.X509Certificates.OpenFl
ags]::MaxAllowed)
$Certexist = ($CertStore.Certificates | where {$_.thumbprint -eq
$Certificate.SignerCertificate.Thumbprint}) -ne $null

if ($Certexist -eq $false)
{
    $CertStore.Add($Certificate.SignerCertificate)
}

$CertStore.Close()
```

As a result, once the certificate is installed, the user should be able to navigate to the Configuration Manager PowerShell drive the next it opens PowerShell and import the Configuration Manager PowerShell module.

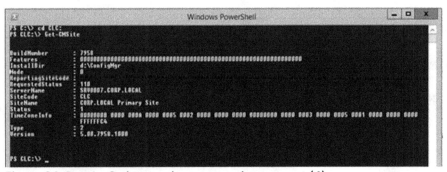

Figure 34. Part I – Script running as a service account (4)

Part II – Warming up

Now that you have learned a bit about PowerShell, WMI and the Configuration Manager PowerShell module, it is time to explore what the Configuration Manager PowerShell cmdlets can do for us and how you can work with it.

Get-CMManagementPoint

To start, let's use the `Get-CMManagementPoint` cmdlet. This cmdlet returns a list of management points.

Note: All command lines and scripts used can be found on the `Part II – 01 – Get-CMManagementPoint.ps1` PowerShell script file

To list all management points, you can use `Get-CMManagementPoint` without any parameter

```
get-cmmanagementpoint
```

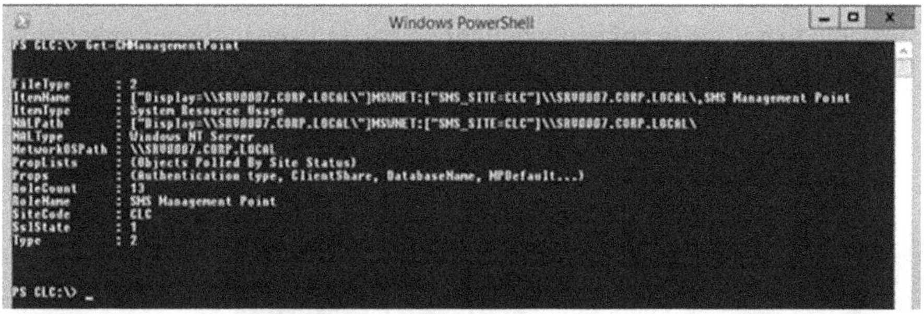

Figure 35. Part II – Get-CMManagementPoint (1)

If you want management points only from a site specific (important for companies that have more than one Configuration Manager site), you can filter it by the `SiteCode` parameter:

```
Get-CMManagementPoint -SiteCode CLC
```

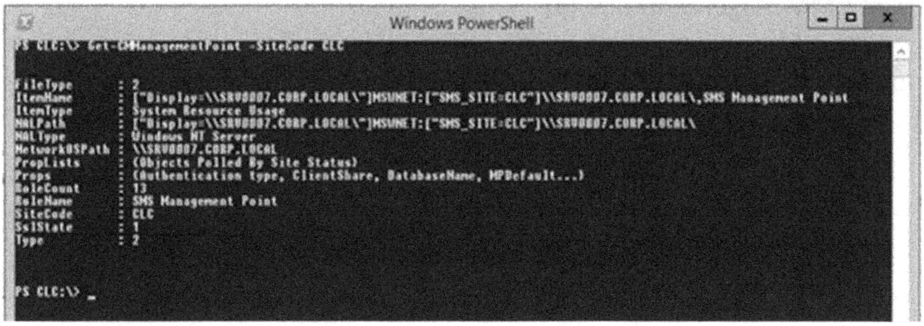

Figure 36. Part II – Get-CMManagementPoint (2)

If you have multiple domains, and want to filter by the domain (imagine the scenario where you have a DMZ). In this case, you could filter by the parameter SiteSystemServerName:

```
Get-CMManagementPoint -SiteSystemServerName *corp.local*
```

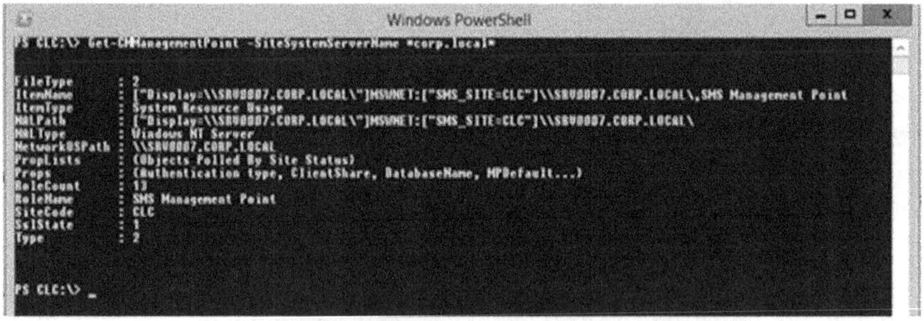

Figure 37. Part II – Get-CMManagementPoint (3)

Note: Using the '*' was removed on the CU2 and re-added on CU3.

So far, you have been able to get the list of management points, but you were not able to use it later on. An easy way to use it later to save to a variable. To do this, you could do:

```
$MPList = Get-CMManagementPoint
```

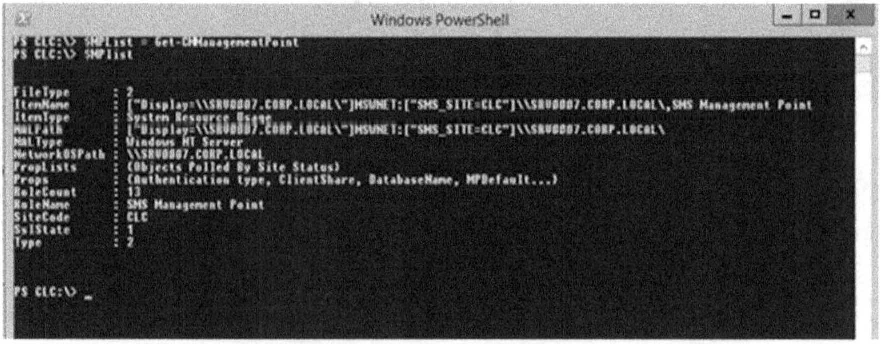

Figure 38. Part II – Get-CMManagementPoint (4)

Now, you could use the $MPList to filter a bit more, maybe you want to know the list of MPs that accept HTTPS connection only. In this example, use:

```
$MPList | Where-Object {$_.SslState -eq 1}
```

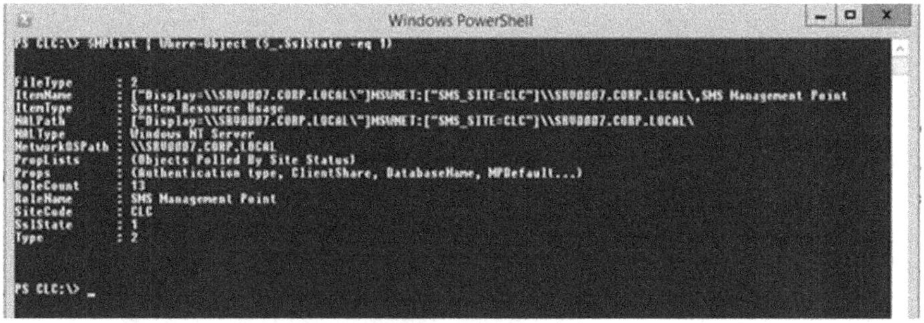

Figure 39. Part II – Get-CMManagementPoint (5)

What about the other properties? Well, PowerShell is intelligent enough to show you only the most common properties. If you want to see all properties, you can use "| select *".

```
$MPList | select *
```

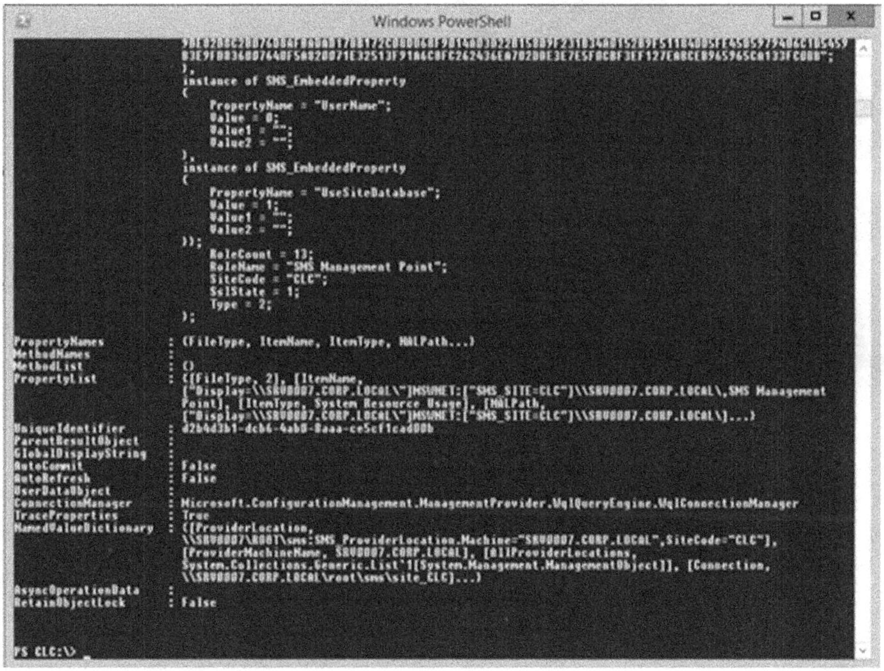

Figure 40. Part II – Get-CMManagementPoint (6)

But what about "Property" and "PropertyLists"? Property and ProperlyList are normally objects inside a property and sometimes referred as lazy properties.

Lazy properties are object properties relatively inefficient to retrieve. If these properties were retrieved for many instances in a class (as might be done in a query), the response would be considerably delayed. Lazy properties and are not usually retrieved during query operations. However, if these properties are retrieved during a query, they have null or zero values, which might not be the actual value of the property for every instance. Therefore, if you want to get the correct value for lazy properties, you must get each instance individually.

When you use the cmdlets, all lazy properties are retrieved, but how to query or use them? You can see all objects inside the props "field" when using:

```
$MPList | %{$_.Props}
```

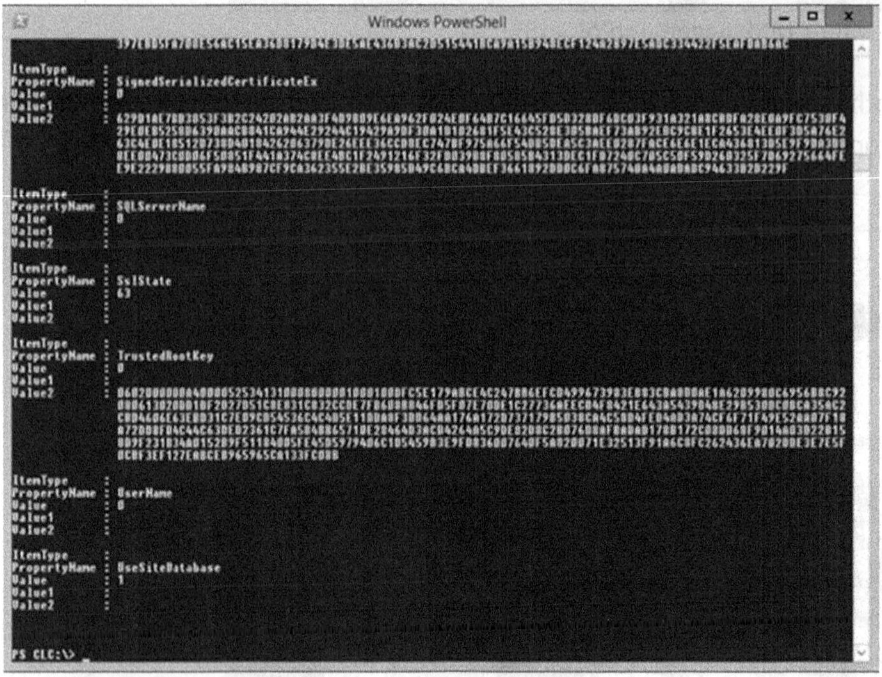

Figure 41. Part II – Get-CMManagementPoint (7)

If you want to know what Management Points are not Internet Facing, how to do it? Would the following command be enough?

```
$MPList | Where-Object { ($_.Props.PropertyName -eq
"MPInternetFacing") -and ($_.Props.Value -eq 0) }
```

Figure 42. Part II – Get-CMManagementPoint (8)

Or maybe using the following command:

```
$MPList.Props | Where-Object {($_.PropertyName -eq
"MPInternetFacing") -and ($_.Value -eq 0)}
```

Figure 43. Part II – Get-CMManagementPoint (9)

This seems to be working; however, it does not allow you to know what the Management Point Name. The best approach would be to list all MP's that are internet facing using foreach and checking its properties

```
foreach ($mp in $mpList) { if (($mp.Props | Where-Object
{($_.PropertyName -eq "MPInternetFacing") -and ($_.Value -eq 0)}) -ne
$null) { $mp } }
```

This command will print all internet facing MP's, regardless of the number of MP's.

Figure 44. Part II – Get-CMManagementPoint (10)

Get-CMApplication

Now, let's play a bit with the `Get-CMApplication` as well as WMI queries and see what are the differences between them. The `Get-CMApplication` cmdlet returns a list of all applications.

Note: All command lines and scripts used can be found on the `Part II – 02 – Get-CMApplication.ps1` PowerShell script file

The `Get-CMApplication` get all properties of an application in Configuration Manager. Without any filtering, it will return all applications and all properties, so it will take a long time.

```
Get-CMApplication
```

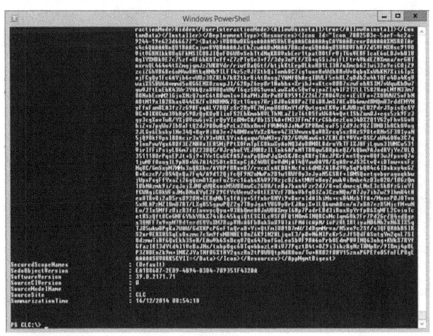

Figure 45. Part II – Get-CMApplication (1)

The equivalent command in WMI would:

```
gwmi -namespace root\sms\site_clc -class SMS_Application
```

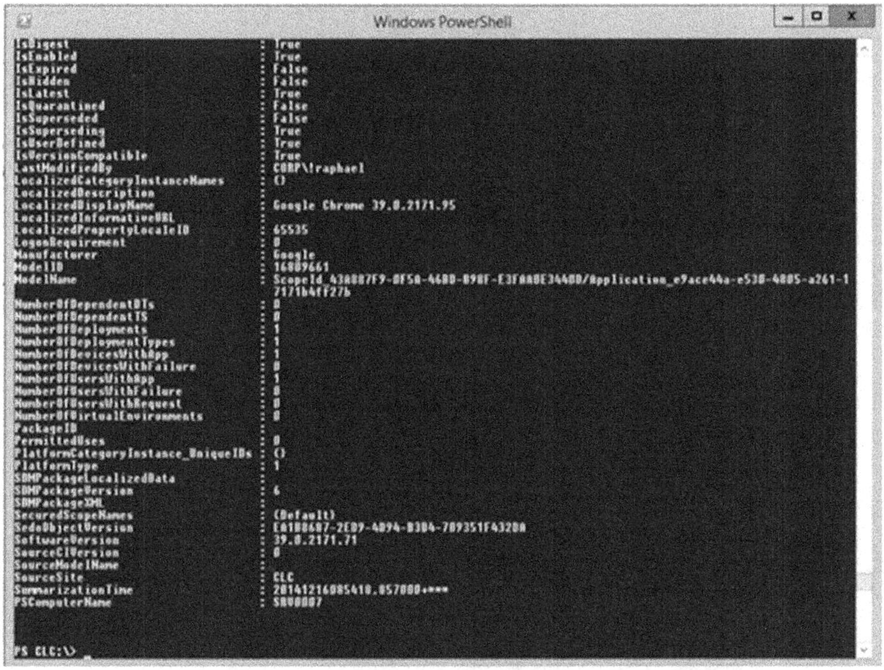

Figure 46. Part II – Get-CMApplication (2)

The main difference between both commands would be the lazy properties, as you can see, connecting to the WMI does not bring the lazy properties while the Get-CMApplication does and because of it, it will be a lot slower as you can see with the following list of commands

```
$Start = Get-Date
$Apps = gwmi -namespace root\sms\site_clc -class SMS_Application
$End = Get-Date
(New-TimeSpan -Start $start -End $end).TotalSeconds
```

Figure 47. Part II – Get-CMApplication (3)

While doing the same in WMI

```
$Start = Get-Date
$Apps = Get-CMApplication
$End = Get-Date
(New-TimeSpan -Start $start -End $end).TotalSeconds
```

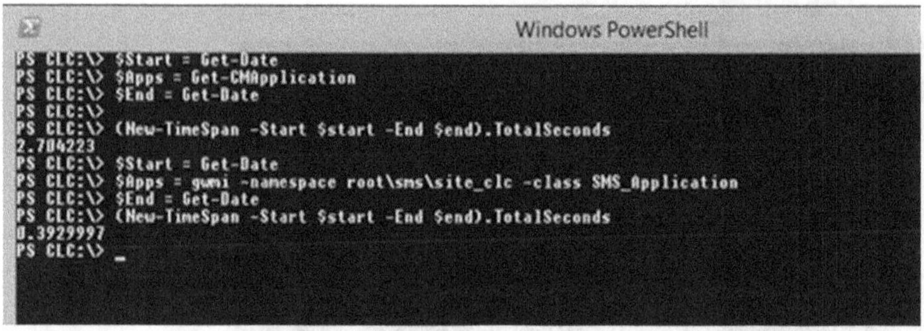

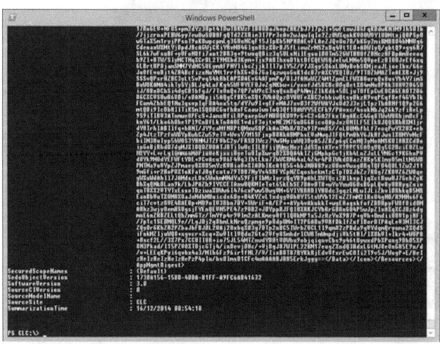

Figure 48. Part II – Get-CMApplication (4)

As you can see, while the Get-CMApplication in this environment took 2.7 seconds, querying the WMI direct took 0.3 seconds. Almost 9 times quicker!

What about filters? If you want to list all applications with Microsoft on its name, use:

```
Get-CMApplication –Name *Microsoft*
```

Figure 49. Part II – Get-CMApplication (5)

As you can see, it is not possible to see the name of the applications. The easiest way to remediate this would be using the "| select LocalizedDisplayName" at the end. The command would be like:

```
Get-CMApplication –Name *Microsoft* | select LocalizedDisplayName
```

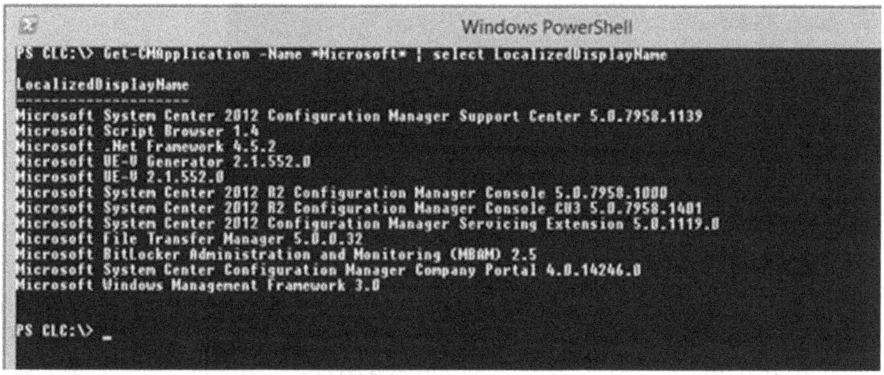

Figure 50. Part II – Get-CMApplication (6)

Similar, you can also filter with WMI, but in this case, you can use 2 options for filter:

```
gwmi -namespace root\sms\site_clc -class SMS_Application -Filter
"LocalizedDisplayName like '%Microsoft%'" | select
LocalizedDisplayName
```

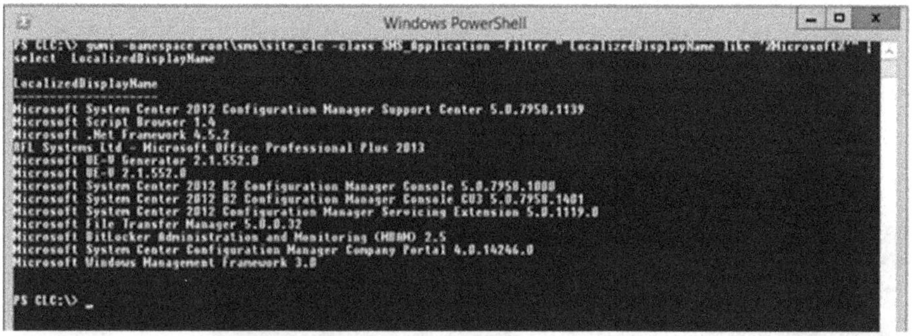

Figure 51. Part II – Get-CMApplication (7)

```
gwmi -namespace root\sms\site_clc -query "select * from
SMS_Application where LocalizedDisplayName like '%Microsoft%'" |
select  LocalizedDisplayName
```

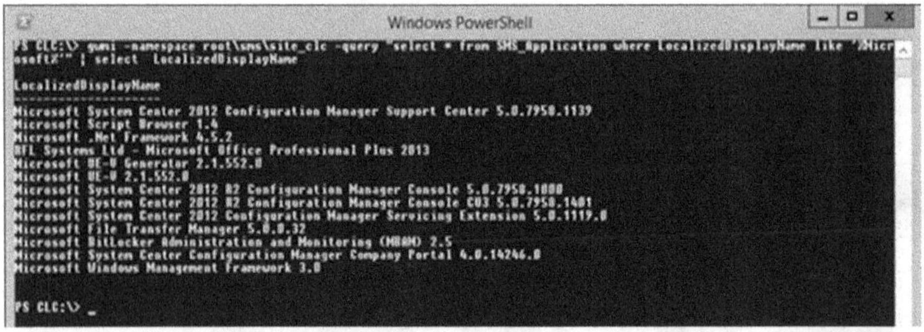

Figure 52. Part II – Get-CMApplication (8)

Now that you know how to see information, let's get a real world example and see what would be the best technology to use. In this example, you would like to see all applications that does not have an Icon associated to it.

Let's start using the Configuration Manager cmdlets

```
$applist = Get-CMApplication
$appList.count
$applist | foreach {
    [xml]$xml = $_.SDMPackageXML
    $icon = $xml.AppMgmtDigest.Application.ChildNodes[0].Info.Icon
    if ($icon -eq $null) { "{0} - {1}" -f $_.LocalizedDisplayName,
($icon -ne $null) }
}
```

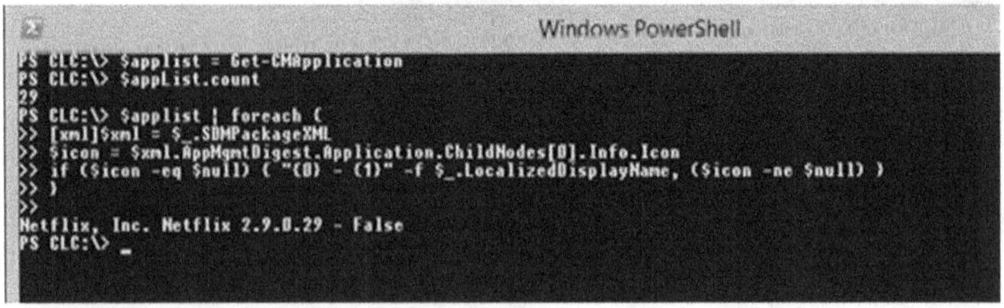

Figure 53. Part II – Get-CMApplication (9)

As you can see, out of 29 applications, 1 does not have the icon associated. And you did this with only 7 lines of code.

What is the equivalent query with WMI? You can easily think that it would be:

```
$applist = gwmi -namespace root\sms\site_clc -class SMS_Application
$appList.count
$applist | foreach {
    $_.Get()
    [xml]$xml = $_.SDMPackageXML
```

```
    $icon = $xml.AppMgmtDigest.Application.ChildNodes[0].Info.Icon
    if ($icon -eq $null) { "{0} - {1}" -f $_.LocalizedDisplayName,
($icon -ne $null) }
}
```

Figure 54. Part II – Get-CMApplication (10)

As you can see, you had to add the Get() method, this is because you need to have access to a lazy property. Another thing to notice is the number of applications. Why there is now 36 applications? This is because the Get-CMApplication does not use the SMS_Application class. Instead, it uses the SMS_ApplicationLatest class as you can see when looking at the log.

Figure 55. Part II – Get-CMApplication (11)

Changing the code to use SMS_ApplicationLatest instead of the SMS_Application should produce the same result

```
$applist = gwmi -namespace root\sms\site_clc -class
SMS_ApplicationLatest
$appList.count
$applist | foreach {
    $_.Get()
    [xml]$xml = $_.SDMPackageXML
    $icon = $xml.AppMgmtDigest.Application.ChildNodes[0].Info.Icon
    if ($icon -eq $null) { "{0} - {1}" -f $_.LocalizedDisplayName,
($icon -ne $null) }
}
```

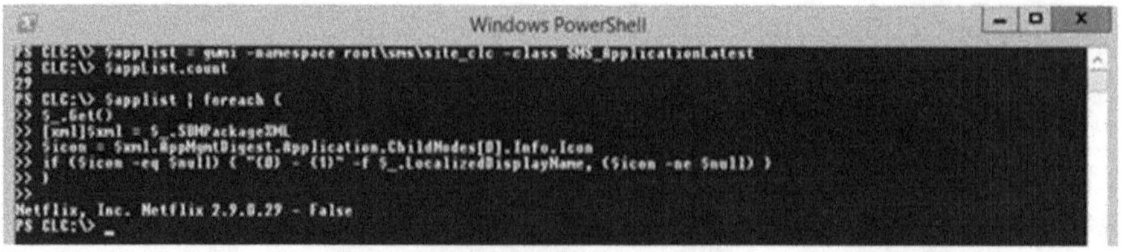

Figure 56. Part II – Get-CMApplication (12)

Now you have the same 29 applications and the same application without an associated icon. Which method is faster? Let's discover…

Using the Get-CMApplication

```
$Start = Get-Date
$applist = Get-CMApplication
$appList.count
$applist | foreach {
    [xml]$xml = $_.SDMPackageXML
    $icon = $xml.AppMgmtDigest.Application.ChildNodes[0].Info.Icon
    if ($icon -eq $null) { "{0} - {1}" -f $_.LocalizedDisplayName,
($icon -ne $null) }
}
$End = Get-Date
(New-TimeSpan -Start $start -End $end).TotalSeconds
```

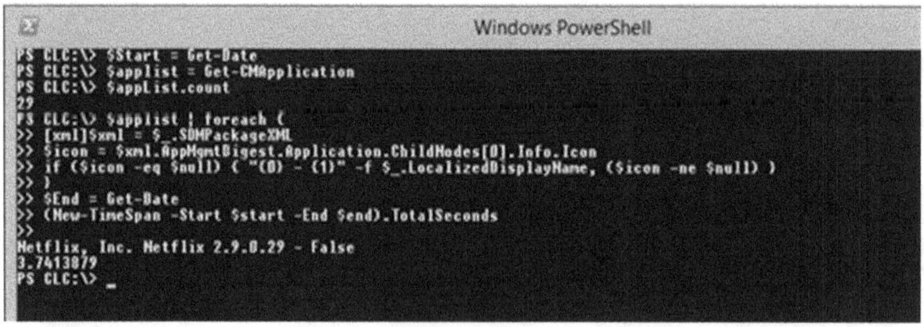

Figure 57. Part II – Get-CMApplication (13)

And using WMI queries

```
$Start = Get-Date
$applist = gwmi -namespace root\sms\site_clc -class
SMS_ApplicationLatest
$appList.count
$applist | foreach {
    $_.Get()
    [xml]$xml = $_.SDMPackageXML
    $icon = $xml.AppMgmtDigest.Application.ChildNodes[0].Info.Icon
    if ($icon -eq $null) { "{0} - {1}" -f $_.LocalizedDisplayName,
($icon -ne $null) }
```

```
}
$End = Get-Date
(New-TimeSpan -Start $start -End $end).TotalSeconds
```

```
                              Windows PowerShell
PS CLC:\> $Start = Get-Date
PS CLC:\> $applist = gwmi -namespace root\sms\site_clc -class SMS_ApplicationLatest
PS CLC:\> $appList.count
29
PS CLC:\> $applist | foreach (
>> $_.Get()
>> [xml]$xml = $_.SDMPackageXML
>> $icon = $xml.AppMgmtDigest.Application.ChildNodes[0].Info.Icon
>> if ($icon -eq $null) { "(0) - (1)" -f $_.LocalizedDisplayName, ($icon -ne $null) )
>> }
>> $End = Get-Date
>> (New-TimeSpan -Start $start -End $end).TotalSeconds
>>
Netflix, Inc. Netflix 2.9.0.29 - False
2.8267267
PS CLC:\> _
```

Figure 58. Part II – Get-CMApplication (14)

As you can see, Get-CMApplication (3.74s) now is only 1.3 times slower than a WMI Query (2.8s).

Get-CMDeploymentType

The Get-CMDeploymentType gets the deployment type information of an application in Configuration Manager. This cmdlet requires at least one filter that is the name or ID of the Application.

Note: All command lines and scripts used can be found on the Part II – 03 – Get-CMDeploymentType.ps1 PowerShell script file

To get the list of all deployment types for an application called "Microsoft System Center 2012 R2 Configuration Manager Console 5.0.7958.1000" you would need to use:

```
Get-CMDeploymentType -ApplicationName "Microsoft System Center 2012
R2 Configuration Manager Console 5.0.7958.1000"
```

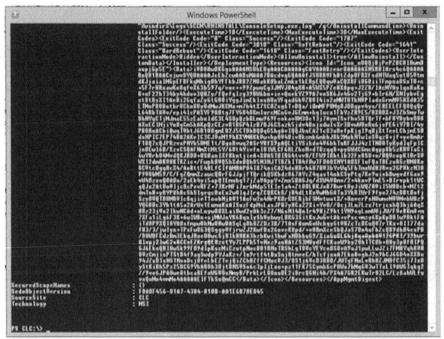

Figure 59. Part II – Get-CMDeploymentType (1)

Conclusion

It is time to flex our scripting muscles and put several cmdlets together. You want a list of all packages of applications that have not yet been distributed to all distribution points on your Configuration Manager hierarchy. Can you accomplish this task easily?

Note: All command lines and scripts used can be found on the `Part II – 04 – Conclusion.ps1` PowerShell script file

First, you need to get a list of all sites in your environment. You can get them with `Get-CMSite` cmdlet:

```
$CMSiteList = Get-CMSite
```

Once it is done, you create a loop with `foreach`. It means that you perform the same tasks for each site and the information of the site will be copied to the `$cmSite` variable. Then you print the site code and the name of the site using the following command:

```
"Site {0} - {1}" -f $cmSite.SiteCode, $cmSite.SiteName
```

Then you get the list of all distribution points connected to the site, using the `Get-CMDistributionPoint` cmdlet and filter any distribution points that has not microsoft.com on its name. You do not want to list the content that is on the cloud distribution point. To accomplish this, use the following command line:

```
$DPList = Get-CMDistributionPoint -SiteCode $cmSite.SiteCode | where-
object {$_.NetworkOSPath -notlike "*microsoft.com"}
```

The next step is to get a list of applications, but only the applications that have any content, using the Get-CMApplication cmdlet. In this example, you can use the Get-CMApplication cmdlet, but a WMI query cloud be used as you have seen before. To accomplish this, use the command line:

```
$AppList = Get-CMApplication | Where-Object {($_.SourceSite -eq
$cmSite.SiteCode) -and ($_.HasContent -eq $true) }
```

Now get the list of the packages with the Get-CMPackage cmdlet (or using the equivalent WMI query). To accomplish this, use the command line:

```
$PkgList = Get-CMPackage | Where-Object {$_.SourceSite -eq
$cmSite.SiteCode }
```

Now you have a list of all distribution points, packages and applications for the site. But, you need to see where the content is missing from.

For the applications, create another loop and inside the loop create another loop for every Distribution Point. Once you have this, you can use a WMI query to validate if the application has been distributed to the distribution points. If the result is empty ($null), print the name of the Application and Distribution Point. You need to perform this query via WMI because there is no equivalent Configuration Manager PowerShell cmdlets. This is accomplished by the following lines:

```
$ContentInfo = gwmi -namespace "root\sms\site_$($cmSite.SiteCode)" -
query "SELECT * FROM SMS_DPContentInfo WHERE NALPath = '$($dp.NALPath
-replace "\\", "\\")' and ObjectType = 512 and ObjectID =
'$($App.ModelName)'"

if ($ContentInfo -eq $null)
{
    "Application {0} missing from {1} " -f $App.LocalizedDisplayName,
$dp.NetworkOSPath
}
```

Then do the same for packages, but instead of using $App.ModelName for objectID use $pkg.PackageID, the same happen for ObjectType where you should use 0 instead of 512.

```
$ContentInfo = gwmi -namespace "root\sms\site_$($cmSite.SiteCode)" -
query "SELECT * FROM SMS_DPContentInfo WHERE NALPath = '$($dp.NALPath
-replace "\\", "\\")' and ObjectType = 0 and ObjectID =
'$($pkg.PackageID)'"

if ($ContentInfo -eq $null)
{
    "Package {0} missing from {1} " -f $Pkg.Name, $dp.NetworkOSPath
}
```

You may be asking yourself, how do you know these numbers? The SDK does have this information available to us:

Figure 60. Part II – Conclusion (1)

And as a result, you might get:

```
Site CLC - CORP.LOCAL Primary Site
Application Microsoft Office Professional Plus 2013 missing from \\SRV0007.CORP.LOCAL
Package User State Migration Tool for Windows 8 missing from \\SRV0007.CORP.LOCAL
Package Monitor Information Reporting missing from \\SRV0007.CORP.LOCAL
Package Recreate machine policy missing from \\SRV0007.CORP.LOCAL
Package KB 3007095 - console update - CLC missing from \\SRV0007.CORP.LOCAL
Package KB 3007095 - x86 client update - CLC missing from \\SRV0007.CORP.LOCAL
Package KB 3007095 - x64 client update - CLC missing from \\SRV0007.CORP.LOCAL
Package KB 3007095 - server update - CLC missing from \\SRV0007.CORP.LOCAL
PS CLC:\>
PS CLC:\>
```

Figure 61. Part II – Conclusion (2)

As you can see, there are many ways you can accomplish the same results. Depending on what you want to accomplish, using WMI may be faster than the native Configuration Manager PowerShell cmdlets. However, using WMI may incur extra time to develop the script as well as extra time for testing.

In real life, you will always use technology you are familiar with and from my experience, I always try to use the Configuration Manager cmdlets before using any other solution as it will be faster to develop. I try to use WMI only when there is no Configuration Manager PowerShell cmdlet available.

Part III – Assets and Compliance

The Assets and Compliance allows you to learn cmdlets that will enable management of the compliance of a Configuration Manager 2012 R2 environment's objects. In this part, you will provide some scripts to allow automation of some of the day-to-day tasks required for a Configuration Manager Administrator or Consultant.

Script 01

Scenario: You are a consultant and you are requested to create collection for each operating system based on location and add a maintenance window.

Note: All command lines and scripts used can be found on the Part III – Assets and Compliance - Script 01.ps1 PowerShell script file

First, you need to set some variables to be used during the script; these variables will hold the following:

- The Configuration Manager Site Code
- The SMS Provider server name
- The list of OS versions and names for workstations and servers
- The limiting collection name

To achieve this, the script has the following lines:

```
$SiteCode = "CLC"
$SDKServer = "SRV0007"
$OSWorkstationArray = @("5.1;Windows XP", "5.2;Windows XP 64-bit
Edition","6.0;Windows Vista", "6.1;Windows 7","6.2;Windows
8","6.3;Windows 8.1")
$OSServerArray = @("5.2;Windows 2003/2003 R2","6.0;Windows 2008",
"6.1;Windows 2008 R2","6.2;Windows 2012","6.3;Windows 2012 R2")
$CollLimit = "All Desktop and Server Clients"
```

Next, import the Configuration Manager PowerShell module if it does not exist for the Site Code and after that, you move to the Configuration Manager site. This is achieved by the following lines:

```
import-module
$env:SMS_ADMIN_UI_PATH.Replace("bin\i386","bin\ConfigurationManager.p
sd1") -force

if ((get-psdrive $SiteCode -erroraction SilentlyContinue |
measure).Count -ne 1)
{
    new-psdrive -Name $SiteCode -PSProvider
"AdminUI.PS.Provider\CMSite" -Root $sdkserver
}
cd "$($SiteCode):"
```

Then you need to identify the AD Site Names that will be used to identify the locations and create 2 schedules, one will be used to perform a full update of the collection and another that will be used by the maintenance window. Both schedules happen on Saturday, the collection update at 9:00pm while the maintenance window starts at 00:00 and is allowed to run 6 hours. To create the schedule, you can use the New-CMSchedule cmdlet. This is achieved by the following lines:

```
$LocationList = gwmi -computername "$sdkserver" -Namespace
"root\sms\site_$sitecode" -query "select distinct ADSiteName from
SMS_R_System where ADSiteName <> ''"
$CollUpdate = New-CMSchedule -Start "01/01/2015 9:00 PM" -DayOfWeek
Saturday -RecurCount 1
$MWSchedule = New-CMSchedule -DayOfWeek Saturday -DurationCount 6 -
DurationInterval Hours -RecurCount 1 -Start "01/01/2015 00:00:00"
```

The next part of the script will run for each Operating System in the $OSWorkstationArray variable. First, you find all operating systems already discovered by Configuration Manager, you do this by querying the WMI class SMS_R_System for all computers that have the Workstation and the version on their name. This is achieved by the following lines:

```
$OSArray = $Os.Split(";")
$OSExist = gwmi -computername "$sdkserver" -Namespace
"root\sms\site_$sitecode" -query "select distinct
OperatingSystemNameandVersion from SMS_R_System where
OperatingSystemNameandVersion like '%Workstation $($OSArray[0])%'"
```

If you find any operating system, you create, if needed, a collection for each location. You do this using the get-CMDeviceCollection and New-CMDeviceCollection cmdlets. After a collection was created, you create the query rule and the maintenance window using the Add-CMDeviceCollectionQueryMembershipRule and New-CMMaintenanceWindow cmdlets. Lastly, you enable the incremental update. However, instead of using a Configuration Manager

PowerShell cmdlet, you update the `RefreshType` property of the WMI instance of the WMI class `SMS_Collection` to 6 (Refresh type indicates how Configuration Manager refreshes the collection. Possible values are MANUAL (1), PERIODIC (2), CONSTANT UPDATE (4) and INCREMENTAL UPDATES (6).). This is achieved by the following lines:

```
$CollectionName = "$($Location.ADSiteName) - $($OSArray[1])"
$Collection = get-CMDeviceCollection -name $CollectionName
if ($Collection -eq $null)
{
    $Collection = New-CMDeviceCollection -Name $CollectionName -
LimitingCollectionName $CollLimit -RefreshSchedule $CollUpdate -
RefreshType Periodic
    $query = "select * from SMS_R_System where
OperatingSystemNameandVersion like '%Workstation $($OSArray[0])%' and
ADSiteName = '$($Location.ADSiteName)'"
    Add-CMDeviceCollectionQueryMembershipRule -CollectionId
$Collection.CollectionID -RuleName "$($OSArray[1])" -QueryExpression
$query
    New-CMMaintenanceWindow -Name ("Saturday 00:00 - 06:00") -
CollectionID $Collection.CollectionID -Schedule $MWSchedule | out-
null

    $WMIColl =
[wmi]"\\$($sdkserver)\root\sms\site_$($sitecode):SMS_Collection.Colle
ctionID='$($Collection.CollectionID)'"
    $WMIColl.RefreshType=6
    $WMIColl.put() | Out-Null
}
```

The next part of the script will run for each Operating System in the `$OSServerArray` variable. First, find all operating systems already discovered by Configuration Manager, by querying the WMI class `SMS_R_System` for all computers that have the server and the version on their name. This is achieved by the following lines:

```
$OSArray = $Os.Split(";")
$OSExist = gwmi -computername "$sdkserver" -Namespace
"root\sms\site_$sitecode" -query "select distinct
OperatingSystemNameandVersion from SMS_R_System where
OperatingSystemNameandVersion like '%Server $($OSArray[0])%'"
```

For any operating system found, a new collection for each location is created with the `get-CMDeviceCollection` and `New-CMDeviceCollection` cmdlets. After the collection is created, create the query rule and the maintenance window using the `Add-CMDeviceCollectionQueryMembershipRule` and `New-CMMaintenanceWindow` cmdlets. Lastly, enable the incremental update. This is done updating the `RefreshType` of the WMI instance of the WMI class `SMS_Collection` to 6. This is achieved by the following lines:

```
$CollectionName = "$($Location.ADSiteName) - $($OSArray[1])"
$Collection = get-CMDeviceCollection -name $CollectionName
if ($Collection -eq $null)
{
    $Collection = New-CMDeviceCollection -Name $CollectionName -
LimitingCollectionName $CollLimit -RefreshSchedule $CollUpdate -
RefreshType Periodic
    $query = "select * from SMS_R_System where
OperatingSystemNameandVersion like '%Workstation $($OSArray[0])%' and
ADSiteName = '$($Location.ADSiteName)'"
    Add-CMDeviceCollectionQueryMembershipRule -CollectionId
$Collection.CollectionID -RuleName "$($OSArray[1])" -QueryExpression
$query
    New-CMMaintenanceWindow -Name ("Saturday 00:00 - 06:00") -
CollectionID $Collection.CollectionID -Schedule $MWSchedule | out-
null

    $WMIColl =
[wmi]"\\$($sdkserver)\root\sms\site_$($sitecode):SMS_Collection.Colle
ctionID='$($Collection.CollectionID)'"
    $WMIColl.RefreshType=6
    $WMIColl.put() | Out-Null
}
```

Note: You may be asking yourself, why using two variables for desktop and servers? There are two reasons, first is the name of the OS for servers is different than workstations and the second is the query. For servers you use the word "Server" and for workstations you use the word "Workstation".

And as a result, you will see all necessary collections created:

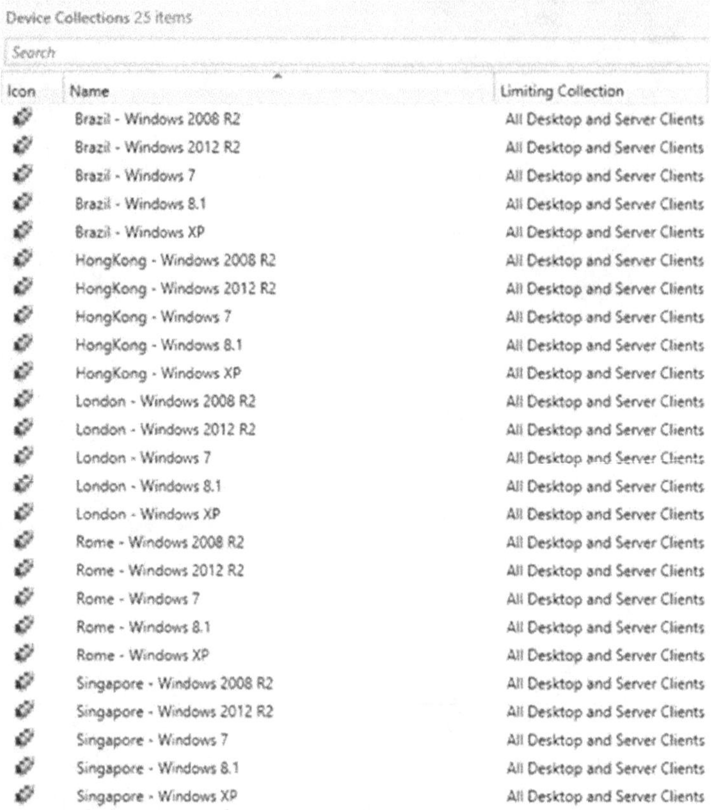

Icon	Name	Limiting Collection
	Brazil - Windows 2008 R2	All Desktop and Server Clients
	Brazil - Windows 2012 R2	All Desktop and Server Clients
	Brazil - Windows 7	All Desktop and Server Clients
	Brazil - Windows 8.1	All Desktop and Server Clients
	Brazil - Windows XP	All Desktop and Server Clients
	HongKong - Windows 2008 R2	All Desktop and Server Clients
	HongKong - Windows 2012 R2	All Desktop and Server Clients
	HongKong - Windows 7	All Desktop and Server Clients
	HongKong - Windows 8.1	All Desktop and Server Clients
	HongKong - Windows XP	All Desktop and Server Clients
	London - Windows 2008 R2	All Desktop and Server Clients
	London - Windows 2012 R2	All Desktop and Server Clients
	London - Windows 7	All Desktop and Server Clients
	London - Windows 8.1	All Desktop and Server Clients
	London - Windows XP	All Desktop and Server Clients
	Rome - Windows 2008 R2	All Desktop and Server Clients
	Rome - Windows 2012 R2	All Desktop and Server Clients
	Rome - Windows 7	All Desktop and Server Clients
	Rome - Windows 8.1	All Desktop and Server Clients
	Rome - Windows XP	All Desktop and Server Clients
	Singapore - Windows 2008 R2	All Desktop and Server Clients
	Singapore - Windows 2012 R2	All Desktop and Server Clients
	Singapore - Windows 7	All Desktop and Server Clients
	Singapore - Windows 8.1	All Desktop and Server Clients
	Singapore - Windows XP	All Desktop and Server Clients

Figure 62. Part III – Assets and Compliance - Script 01 (1)

Script 02

Scenario: You are a consultant and for Operating System Deployment, you need to import a list of devices (if they do not exist) and set the primary user based on a CSV file given by someone else.

Note: All command lines and scripts used can be found on the `Part III – Assets and Compliance - Script 02.ps1` PowerShell script file

First, you need to set some variables to be used during the script; these variables will hold the following:

- The Configuration Manager Site Code
- The SMS Provider server name
- File name of a CSV file with the format as: computer name, mac address, primary users (when there is multiple primary users, you use ";" to identify them). The MAC address is not required if the machine is an existing Configuration Manager machine
- Load the CSV file into a variable

To achieve this, the script has the following lines:

```
$SiteCode = "CLC"
$SDKServer = "SRV0007"
$filename = "c:\temp\computerinfo.csv"
$compList = gc $filename
```

Next, import the Configuration Manager PowerShell module if it does not exist for the Site Code and after that, you move to the Configuration Manager site. This is achieved by the following lines:

```
import-module
$env:SMS_ADMIN_UI_PATH.Replace("bin\i386","bin\ConfigurationManager.p
sd1") -force

if ((get-psdrive $SiteCode -erroraction SilentlyContinue |
measure).Count -ne 1)
{
    new-psdrive -Name $SiteCode -PSProvider
"AdminUI.PS.Provider\CMSite" -Root $sdkserver
}
cd "$($SiteCode):"
```

The next part of the script will run for each line found in the CSV file. Once you know the computer information, populate some variables for better identify the computer information. This is achieved by the following lines:

```
$compArray = $computer.Split(",")
$ComputerName = $compArray[0]
$MacAddress = $compArray[1]
$PrimaryUsers = $compArray[2].Split(";")
```

Next step is to check if the computer exist in the Configuration Manager database using the get-cmdevice cmdlet. This is achieved by the following lines:

```
$CMComputerInfo = get-cmdevice -name "$computerName"
```

If the computer does not exist and the MAC address is used on the CSV file, import the computer information to the All Systems collection using the Import-CMComputerInformation cmdlet. This is achieved by the following lines:

```
if ($MacAddress -eq "") { continue }
$CMComputerInfo = Import-CMComputerInformation -CollectionName "All
Systems" -ComputerName "$ComputerName" -MacAddress "$MacAddress"
```

If the computer exist, you remove any Primary User, first, you get all primary users assigned to the device and then remove it. Use the get-cmuserdeviceaffinity and remove-CMDeviceAffinityFromUser cmdlets. This is achieved by the following lines:

```
get-cmuserdeviceaffinity -DeviceName "$ComputerName" | foreach {
remove-CMDeviceAffinityFromUser -DeviceName "$ComputerName" -UserName
$_.UniqueUserName }
```

Then it is time to add the new Primary users to the computer and you do the operation for each primary user on the CSV file. First, validate if the user exist in the Configuration Manager database and in case it exists, create the affinity with get-cmuser and Add-CMDeviceAffinityToUser cmdlets. This is achieved by the following lines:

```
if ($user -eq "") { continue }
$userinfo = get-cmuser -name "$user"
if ($userinfo -ne $null)
{
    Add-CMDeviceAffinityToUser -username "$user" -DeviceName
"$ComputerName"
}
```

Note: Once the script import the computer information, there is a delay of 10 seconds that should be enough for Configuration Manager to finish processing the data. However, depending on the environment this may not be enough. If it is the case, you will noticed that the primary users are not assigned to the computer.

And as a result, you would see the primary users assigned to the device

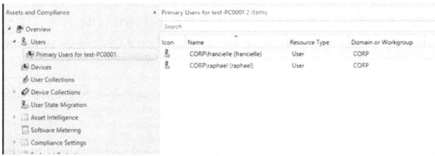

Figure 63. Part III – Assets and Compliance - Script 02 (1)

Script 03

Scenario: You are a consultant and you need to configure the Power Management feature for collections. Those collections are using the same custom settings, but various time intervals or values are different for each collection. They are currently stored on a CSV file by someone else.

Note: All command lines and scripts used can be found on the `Part III – Assets and Compliance - Script 03.ps1` PowerShell script file

First, you need to set some variables to be used during the script; these variables will hold the following:

- The Configuration Manager Site Code
- The SMS Provider server name
- File name of a CSV file with the format as: Collection Name, Peak Start Time, Peak End Time, Wake Up Time (if the collection does not need this information, it can be empty)
- Name and description of the Peak and Non-Peak power management

To achieve this, the script has the following lines:

```
$SiteCode = "CLC"
$SDKServer = "SRV0007"
$FileName = "c:\temp\PowerConfig.csv"
##CollectionName,StartTime,EndTime,WakeUpTime
$powerlist = gc $FileName
$NonPeakName = "Customized Non-peak (Configuration Manager)"
$NonPeakDesc = "Configured by the IT department via Configuration
Manager"
$PeakName = "Customized Peak (Configuration Manager)"
$PeakDesc = "Configured by the IT department via Configuration
Manager"
```

Once the variables are set, it is time to set the Peak and non-Peak power plan. They ID's are stored on an array with the settings when the device is connected to power and connected to the battery. To achieve this, the script has the following lines:

```
$PeakPlan = @('3c0bc021-c8a8-4e07-a973-6b14cbcb2b7e,1200,600',
'29f6c1db-86da-48c5-9fdb-f2b67b1f44da,3600,900',
'0e796bdb-100d-47d6-a2d5-f7d2daa51f51,1,1',
'7648efa3-dd9c-4e3e-b566-50f929386280,1,1',
'a7066653-8d6c-40a8-910e-a1f54b84c7e5,0,0',
'96996bc0-ad50-47ec-923b-6f41874dd9eb,1,1',
'5ca83367-6e45-459f-a27b-476b1d01c936,1,1',
'6738e2c4-e8a5-4a42-b16a-e040e769756e,1200,300',
'9d7815a6-7ee4-497e-8888-515a05f02364,0,0',
```

```
'd8742dcb-3e6a-4b3c-b3fe-374623cdcf06,0,0',
'637ea02f-bbcb-4015-8e2c-a1c7b9c0b546,0,2',
'81cd32e0-7833-44f3-8737-7081f38d1f70,0,0',
'bd3b718a-0680-4d9d-8ab2-e1d2b4ac806d,1,1'
)

$NonPeakPlan = @('3c0bc021-c8a8-4e07-a973-6b14cbcb2b7e,1200,600',
'29f6c1db-86da-48c5-9fdb-f2b67b1f44da,3600,900',
'0e796bdb-100d-47d6-a2d5-f7d2daa51f51,1,1',
'7648efa3-dd9c-4e3e-b566-50f929386280,1,1',
'a7066653-8d6c-40a8-910e-a1f54b84c7e5,0,0',
'96996bc0-ad50-47ec-923b-6f41874dd9eb,1,1',
'5ca83367-6e45-459f-a27b-476b1d01c936,1,1',
'6738e2c4-e8a5-4a42-b16a-e040e769756e,1200,300',
'9d7815a6-7ee4-497e-8888-515a05f02364,0,0',
'd8742dcb-3e6a-4b3c-b3fe-374623cdcf06,0,0',
'637ea02f-bbcb-4015-8e2c-a1c7b9c0b546,0,2',
'81cd32e0-7833-44f3-8737-7081f38d1f70,0,0',
'bd3b718a-0680-4d9d-8ab2-e1d2b4ac806d,1,1'
)
```

Note: Each GUID represent a power management setting. A description of what they do, can be found running the following command line in a PowerShell console.

```
powercfg /query | foreach { $value = $_ ; if ($value.IndexOf("Power
Setting GUID") -ge 0) { write-host $value } }
```

Note: Configuration Manager does not support all GUIDs that windows support, the list of GUIDs can be found enabling all settings on a test collection and running the following PowerShell commands:

```
$CollName = "Name of Collection with Power Management Settings"
$collection = Get-CMDeviceCollection -name "$($CollName)"
$CollectionSettings = Get-WmiObject -ComputerName "$($SDKServer)" -
Class "SMS_CollectionSettings" -Namespace
"root\SMS\site_$($SiteCode)" -Filter
"CollectionId='$($Collection.CollectionId)'"
$CollectionSettings.Get()
([xml]$CollectionSettings.PowerConfigs[0].PeakPowerPlan).PowerScheme.
PowerSettings.PowerSetting
```

Next, import the Configuration Manager PowerShell module if it does not exist for the Site Code and after that, you move to the Configuration Manager site. This is achieved by the following lines:

```
import-module
$env:SMS_ADMIN_UI_PATH.Replace("bin\i386","bin\ConfigurationManager.p
sd1") -force

if ((get-psdrive $SiteCode -erroraction SilentlyContinue |
measure).Count -ne 1)
{
    new-psdrive -Name $SiteCode -PSProvider
"AdminUI.PS.Provider\CMSite" -Root $sdkserver
}
cd "$($SiteCode):"
```

Then it is time to create the XML string for the peak and non-peak power plan. You do this for all elements of the $NonPeakPlan and $PeakPlan power plan array.

```
$NonPeakXML = ""
foreach ($setting in $NonPeakPlan)
{
    $array = $setting.Split(",")
    $NonPeakXML +=
'<PowerSetting><GUID>'+$array[0]+'</GUID><CurrentACPowerSettingIndex>
'+$array[1]+'</CurrentACPowerSettingIndex><CurrentDCPowerSettingIndex
>'+$array[2]+'</CurrentDCPowerSettingIndex></PowerSetting>'
}
$NonPeakXML = '<?xml version="1.0" encoding="utf-16"?><PowerScheme
xmlns:xsi="http://www.w3.org/2001/XMLSchema-instance"
xmlns:xsd="http://www.w3.org/2001/XMLSchema" GUID="db310065-829b-
4671-9647-2261c00e86ef" Name="' + $NonPeakName + '" Description="' +
$NonPeakDesc
+'"><PowerSettings>'+$NonPeakXML+'</PowerSettings></PowerScheme>'

$PeakXML = ""
foreach ($setting in $PeakPlan)
{
    $array = $setting.Split(",")
    $PeakXML +=
'<PowerSetting><GUID>'+$array[0]+'</GUID><CurrentACPowerSettingIndex>
'+$array[1]+'</CurrentACPowerSettingIndex><CurrentDCPowerSettingIndex
>'+$array[2]+'</CurrentDCPowerSettingIndex></PowerSetting>'
}
$PeakXML = '<?xml version="1.0" encoding="utf-16"?><PowerScheme
xmlns:xsi="http://www.w3.org/2001/XMLSchema-instance"
xmlns:xsd="http://www.w3.org/2001/XMLSchema" GUID="db310065-829b-
4671-9647-2261c00e86ef" Name="' + $PeakName + '" Description="' +
$PeakDesc +
'"><PowerSettings>'+$PeakXML+'</PowerSettings></PowerScheme>'
```

The next part of the script will run for each line found in the CSV file. Once you know the collection name, you check to confirm that the collection exist and if it does exist, you get the extra information needed that is stored on the WMI SMS_CollectionSettings class. Unfortunately, there is no PowerShell cmdlet available at the moment. This is achieved by the following lines:

```
$PowerMgmtarray = $PowerMgmt.Split(",")
$collection = Get-CMDeviceCollection -name "$($PowerMgmtarray[0])"
if ($Collection -eq $null) { continue }
$CollectionSettings = Get-WmiObject -ComputerName "$($SDKServer)" -
Class "SMS_CollectionSettings" -Namespace
"root\SMS\site_$($SiteCode)" -Filter
"CollectionId='$($Collection.CollectionId)'"
$CollectionSettings.Get()
```

Next step is to check if there is already a power plan set up for the collection and if it exist, you remove it. This is achieved by the following lines:

```
if ($CollectionSettings.PowerConfigs.Count -ne 0)
{
    $CollectionSettings.PowerConfigs = @()
}
```

Once you have cleared the existing policy (if one exist), you add the new information using an instance of the WMI SMS_PowerConfig class. This is achieved by the following lines:

```
$PowerConfig = ([WMIClass]
"\\$SDKServer\root\SMS\site_$($SiteCode):SMS_PowerConfig").CreateInst
ance()
$PowerConfig.ConfigID = $Collection.CollectionId
$PowerConfig.DurationInSec = (([datetime]$PowerMgmtarray[2])-
([datetime]$PowerMgmtarray[1])).TotalSeconds
$PowerConfig.PeakStartTimeHoursMin = $PowerMgmtarray[1]
$PowerConfig.WakeUpTimeHoursMin = $PowerMgmtarray[3]
$PowerConfig.NonPeakPowerPlan = $NonPeakXML
$PowerConfig.PeakPowerPlan = $PeakXML
$CollectionSettings.PowerConfigs += $PowerConfig.psobject.BaseObject
```

Lastly, you save the object using the WMI Put() method. This is achieved by the following lines:

```
$CollectionSettings.Put()
```

And as a result, you would see the collection with the new (or updated) Power Management Settings

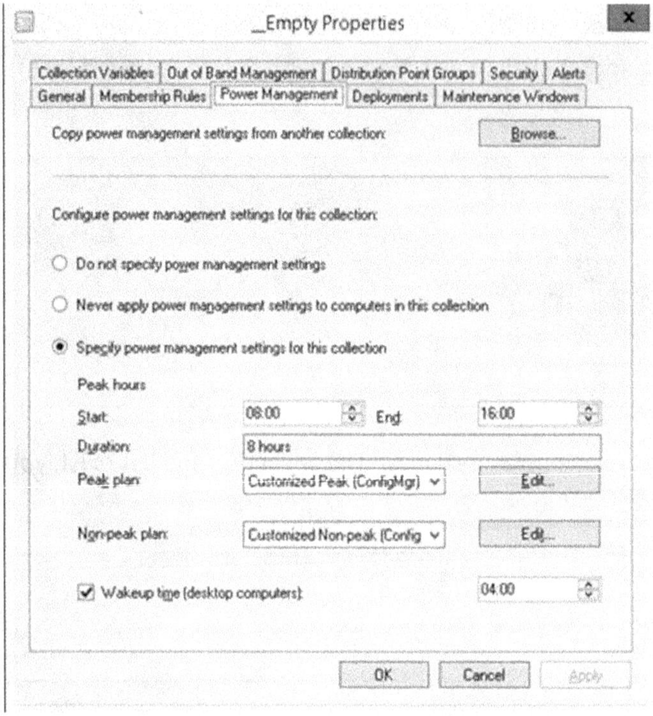

Figure 64. Part III – Assets and Compliance - Script 03 (1)

Script 04

Scenario: You are a consultant and need to create a Compliance Settings Baseline based on the software upgrades group.

Note: All command lines and scripts used can be found on the `Part III – Assets and Compliance - Script 04.ps1` PowerShell script file

First, you need to set some variables to be used during the script; these variables will hold the following:

- The Configuration Manager Site Code
- The SMS Provider server name
- The beginning of the name of the baseline

To achieve this, the script has the following lines:

```
$SiteCode = "CLC"
$SDKServer = "SRV0007"
$BeginingOftheName = "Software Updates"
```

Next, import the Configuration Manager PowerShell module if it does not exist for the Site Code and after that, you move to the Configuration Manager site. This is achieved by the following lines:

```
import-module
$env:SMS_ADMIN_UI_PATH.Replace("bin\i386","bin\ConfigurationManager.p
sd1") -force

if ((get-psdrive $SiteCode -erroraction SilentlyContinue |
measure).Count -ne 1)
{
    new-psdrive -Name $SiteCode -PSProvider
"AdminUI.PS.Provider\CMSite" -Root $sdkserver
}
cd "$($SiteCode):"
```

Then it is time to get a list of all Software Update groups with the `Get-CMSoftwareUpdateGroup` cmdlet. This is achieved by the following lines:

```
$SwUpdateGroupList = Get-CMSoftwareUpdateGroup
```

The next part of the script will run for each Software Update Group found. The first part is to create the baseline name, get the baseline unique ID and get the list of updates and if there is no updates, stop and pass to the next software update group. This is achieved by the following lines:

```
$BaselineName = "$($BeginingOftheName) -
$($SUPGroup.LocalizedDisplayName)"
$SUPGroupID = $SUPGroup.CI_ID

$updates = gwmi -computername $sdkserver -Namespace
"root\sms\site_$SiteCode" -query "SELECT upd.* FROM
SMS_SoftwareUpdate upd, SMS_CIRelation cr WHERE cr.FromCIID=
$SUPGroupID AND cr.RelationType=1 AND upd.CI_ID=cr.ToCIID"
if ($updates.Length -le 0) { Continue }
```

Next step is to check if the baseline exist and if not, create one. You can accomplish the creation with the Get-CMBaseline and New-CMBaseline cmdlets. This is achieved by the following lines:

```
$Baseline = Get-CMBaseline -Name "$BaselineName"
if ($Baseline -eq $null)
{
    $Baseline = New-CMBaseline -Name "$BaselineName"
}
```

Once you have the baseline information, you get the version number and create an increment it as well as you get the xml definition. This is necessary because Configuration Manager keeps a history of all changes and because there is no built-in cmdlets to add Software Update to a compliance settings baseline. This is achieved by the following lines:

```
$BaselineVersion = $Baseline.SDMPackageVersion
$BaselineNewVersion = $Baseline.SDMPackageVersion + 1
[xml]$baselinexmldef = Get-CMBaselineXMLDefinition -name
"$BaselineName"
```

Once you have the version and the xml, you clear the existing baseline software update information, if exist and create a variable to hold the replace string that will be used later. This is achieved by the following lines:

```
if
($baselinexmldef.DesiredConfigurationDigest.Baseline.SoftwareUpdates
-ne "")
{

$baselinexmldef.DesiredConfigurationDigest.Baseline.SoftwareUpdates.R
emoveAll()
    $replace = "<SoftwareUpdates></SoftwareUpdates>"
}
else { $replace = "<SoftwareUpdates />" }
```

Then it is time to create the xml for each software update. This is achieved by the following lines:

```
$baselineXML = ""
foreach($upd in $updates)
{
    $ModelName =
$upd.ModelName.Substring(0,$upd.ModelName.IndexOf("/"))
    $LogicalName =
$upd.ModelName.Substring($upd.ModelName.IndexOf("/")+1)
    $baselineXML += '<SoftwareUpdateBundleReference
AuthoringScopeId="'+$ModelName+'" LogicalName="'+$LogicalName+'" />'
}
```

Once you have the software update xml created, replace the existing one and change the version of the baseline. This is achieved by the following lines:

```
$baselineXML = $baselinexmldef.OuterXml.Replace($replace,
"<SoftwareUpdates>$($baselineXML)</SoftwareUpdates>")
$baselineXML =
$baselineXML.Replace('Version="'+$BaselineVersion+'"><Annotation','Ve
rsion="'+$BaselineNewVersion+'"><Annotation')
```

Lastly, you get the Baseline WMI object and change the xml and save, using the WMI `Put()` method. This is required because until now you have been using the PowerShell object. This is achieved by the following lines:

```
$WMIBaseline = gwmi -computername "$sdkserver" -Namespace
"root\sms\site_$SiteCode" -query "SELECT * FROM SMS_ConfigurationItem
where CI_ID = $($Baseline.CI_ID)"
$WMIBaseline.SDMPackageXML = $baselineXML
$WMIBaseline.Put()
```

And as a result, you would see the compliance settings created for all software update groups.

Figure 65. Part III – Assets and Compliance - Script 04 (1)

Script 05

Scenario: You are a consultant and you need to create a list of Software Metering rules (if they do not exist) for the main paid applications used by the company.

Note: All command lines and scripts used can be found on the `Part III - Assets and Compliance - Script 05.ps1` PowerShell script file

First, you need to set some variables to be used during the script; these variables will hold the following:

- The Configuration Manager Site Code
- The SMS Provider server name
- File name of a CSV file with the format as: ProductName, FileName, OriginalFileName, Version (use * for any version), LanguageID (use 0 for any language otherwise, refer to http://go.microsoft.com/fwlink/?LinkId=262651 - use column HexLCID), Comments
- Load the CSV file into a variable

To achieve this, the script has the following lines:

```
$SiteCode = "CLC"
$SDKServer = "SRV0007"
$filename = "c:\temp\rules.csv"
$ruleList = gc $filename
```

Next, import the Configuration Manager PowerShell module if it does not exist for the Site Code and after that, you move to the Configuration Manager site. This is achieved by the following lines:

```
import-module
$env:SMS_ADMIN_UI_PATH.Replace("bin\i386","bin\ConfigurationManager.p
sd1") -force

if ((get-psdrive $SiteCode -erroraction SilentlyContinue |
measure).Count -ne 1)
{
    new-psdrive -Name $SiteCode -PSProvider
"AdminUI.PS.Provider\CMSite" -Root $sdkserver
}
cd "$($SiteCode):"
```

The next part of the script will run for each line found in the CSV file. Once you know the rule information, populate some variables for better identify the rule to be created. This is achieved by the following lines:

```
$rule = $ruleinfo.Split(",")
$ProductName = $rule[0]
$fileName = $rule[1]
$OriginalFileName = $rule[2]
$FileVersion = $rule[3]
$LanguageId = $rule[4]
$Comment = $rule[5]
```

Next step is to check if the rule exist in the Configuration Manager database or not using the `Get-CMSoftwareMeteringRule` cmdlet. This is achieved by the following lines:

```
$CMRule = Get-CMSoftwareMeteringRule -ProductName $ProductName
```

If the rule does not exist, create a new rule using the `New-CMSoftwareMeteringRule` cmdlet. This is achieved by the following lines:

```
$cmrule = New-CMSoftwareMeteringRule -SiteCode "$SiteCode" -
ProductName "$ProductName" -Comment "$Comment" -FileName "$fileName"
-FileVersion "$FileVersion" -OriginalFileName "$OriginalFileName" -
LanguageId $LanguageId
```

The next step is to validate if the rule is enabled or not, and if it is not enabled, you need to enable it. Check the property Enabled and if it is equal to $false, the rule is not enabled. Enable it using the `Enable-CMSoftwareMeteringRule` cmdlet. This is achieved by the following lines:

```
if ($cmrule.Enabled -eq $false)
{
    Enable-CMSoftwareMeteringRule -ProductName $ProductName
}
```

And as a result, you would see all the metering rules created

Icon	Name	Original File Name	File Name	File Version	Language	Enabled
	Adobe Acrobat 11	Acrobat.exe	Acrobat.exe	*		Yes
	Microsoft Visio	Visio.exe	Visio.exe	*		Yes
	Microsoft Project	WINPROJ.EXE	WINPROJ.E...	*		Yes
	Snagit	SNAGIT32.EXE	Snagit32.exe	*		Yes
	Visual Studio 2013 Pro	devenv.exe	devenv.exe	*		Yes

Figure 66. Part III – Assets and Compliance - Script 05 (1)

Part IV – Software Library

The Software Library allows you to learn cmdlets that will enable management of software that will be deployed to a Configuration Manager 2012 R2 environment. In this part, you will provide you some scripts to allow you automated some of the day-to-day tasks required for a Configuration Manager Administrator or Consultant.

The following sections have a selection of scripts that have proven to save time and automation day-to-day tasks in a Configuration Manager environment

Script 01

Scenario: You are a consultant and you need to import an Operating System Image and create a build & capture task sequence.

Note: All command lines and scripts used can be found on the `Part IV - Software Library - Script 01.ps1` PowerShell script file

First, you need to set some variables to be used during the script; these variables will hold the following:

- The Configuration Manager Site Code
- The SMS Provider server name
- Location of the OS File (WIM)
- Operating System Name
- Distribution Point Group Name
- Boot Image
- Configuration Manager Client Package Name
- New computer local administrator password
- Collection Name to deploy the task sequence
- Location where to capture the gold image
- Username/password of the capture share

To achieve this, the script has the following lines:

```
$SiteCode = "CLC"
$SDKServer = "SRV0007"
$wimFile = '\\server\Share\Windows 8.1 EE RTM.wim'
$OSName = "Windows 8.1 x64 Enterprise"
$DPGroupName = "Headquarters"
$BootImageName = "Boot image (x64)"
$ClientPackageName = "Configuration Manager Client Package"
$LocalAdminPwd = 'Pa$$w0rd'| ConvertTo-SecureString -AsPlainText -
Force
$CaptureTO = '\\Server\Share\Windows 8.1 Gold.wim'
$CollectionName = "All Unknown Computers"
$Username = 'domain\username'
$Password = 'Pa$$w0rd'| ConvertTo-SecureString -AsPlainText -Force
```

Note: Because passwords used by the Task Sequence need to be encrypted, you need to convert the passwords using `ConvertTo-SecureScript` cmdlet. As best practices, you should use `Read-Host` cmdlet instead of passing the password as plain text on your script.

Next, import the Configuration Manager PowerShell module if it does not exist for the Site Code and after that, you move to the Configuration Manager site. This is achieved by the following lines:

```
import-module
$env:SMS_ADMIN_UI_PATH.Replace("bin\i386","bin\ConfigurationManager.p
sd1") -force

if ((get-psdrive $SiteCode -erroraction SilentlyContinue |
measure).Count -ne 1)
{
    new-psdrive -Name $SiteCode -PSProvider
"AdminUI.PS.Provider\CMSite" -Root $sdkserver
}
cd "$($SiteCode):"
```

The next part of the script will check if the Operating System Image already exist, and if not, will import the WIM file using `Get-CMOperatingSystemImage` and `New-CMoperatingSystemImage`. This is achieved by the following lines:

```
$OSImage = Get-CMOperatingSystemImage -Name "$OSName"
if ($OSImage -eq $null)
{
    $OSImage = New-CMoperatingSystemImage -Name "$OSName" -path
"$wimFile" -Version "0.1"
}
```

Once you have the Operating System Image, it is time to get the boot image and Configuration Manager client package information using `Get-CMBootImage` and `Get-CMPackage`. This is achieved by the following lines:

```
$Boot = Get-CMBootImage -name $BootImageName

$ClientPackage = Get-CMPackage -name $ClientPackageName
```

Now let's create a new Task Sequence using the `New-CMTaskSequence` cmdlet. The Task Sequence will add the computer to a workgroup, install all windows updates and set the local administrator password. Once the machine has been installed, it will be captured. This is achieved by the following lines:

```
$TaskSequence = New-CMTaskSequence -BootImagePackageId
$boot.PackageID `
-BuildOperatingSystemImageOption `
-JoinDomain WorkgroupType `
-OperatingSystemFileAccount $Username `
-OperatingSystemFileAccountPassword $Password `
-OperatingSystemFilePath $captureTo `
-OperatingSystemImageIndex 1 `
-OperatingSystemImagePackageId $osimage.PackageID `
-TaskSequenceName "Build & Capture $($OSName)" `
-ClientPackagePackageId $ClientPackage.PackageID `
-GeneratePassword $False `
-LocalAdminPassword $LocalAdminPwd `
-SoftwareUpdateStyle All `
-WorkgroupName Workgroup
```

After the task sequence has been created, you can distribute the content to a distribution point group using the `Start-CMContentDistribution` cmdlet. This is achieved by the following lines:

```
Start-CMContentDistribution -DistributionPointGroupName $DPGroupName
-TaskSequenceId $TaskSequence.PackageID
```

Lastly, you need to deploy our task sequence to a collection. It will be deploying it as available and only when the client connects via PXE or Media. Deploy it using the `Start-CMTaskSequenceDeployment` cmdlet. This is achieved by the following lines:

```
Start-CMTaskSequenceDeployment -TaskSequencePackageId
$TaskSequence.PackageID -CollectionName $CollectionName -
Deploypurpose "Available" -MakeAvailableTo "MediaAndPXE"
```

And as a result, you would see the task sequence being deployed to the collection

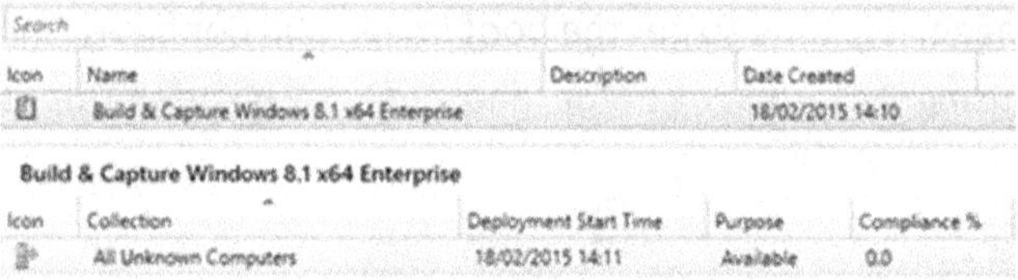

Icon	Name	Description	Date Created
	Search		
	Build & Capture Windows 8.1 x64 Enterprise		18/02/2015 14:10

Build & Capture Windows 8.1 x64 Enterprise

Icon	Collection	Deployment Start Time	Purpose	Compliance %
	All Unknown Computers	18/02/2015 14:11	Available	0.0

Figure 67. Part IV – Software Library - Script 01 (1)

Script 02

Scenario: You are a consultant and you need to create Applications for iOS that are from the Apple Store.

Note: All command lines and scripts used can be found on the Part IV - Software Library - Script 02.ps1 PowerShell script file

First, you need to set some variables to be used during the script; these variables will hold the following:

- The Configuration Manager Site Code
- The SMS Provider server name
- File name of a CSV file with the format as one iTunes URL per line
- Load some .Net assemblies
- Load the URL into a variable

To achieve this, the script has the following lines:

```
$SiteCode = "CLC"
$SDKServer = "SRV0007"
$filename = "c:\temp\iosapp.csv"

[void][System.Reflection.Assembly]::LoadWithPartialName("System.Web")
[void][System.Reflection.Assembly]::LoadWithPartialName("System.Drawing")
$urlList = gc $filename
```

Next, import the Configuration Manager PowerShell module if it does not exist for the Site Code and after that, you move to the Configuration Manager site. This is achieved by the following lines:

```
import-module
$env:SMS_ADMIN_UI_PATH.Replace("bin\i386","bin\ConfigurationManager.psdl") -force

if ((get-psdrive $SiteCode -erroraction SilentlyContinue |
measure).Count -ne 1)
{
    new-psdrive -Name $SiteCode -PSProvider
"AdminUI.PS.Provider\CMSite" -Root $sdkserver
}
cd "$($SiteCode):"
```

The next part of the script will run for each URL you added to the list. Once you know the URL, you try to capture the Name, Publisher, Category and Icon from the URL. The icon is then downloaded to a temporary location and converted to a 250x250 size. This is achieved by the following lines:

```
$r = Invoke-WebRequest $url

$Name = $r.RawContent.Substring($r.RawContent.indexof("<div
id=""title"" class=""intro"),2000)
$Name = $name.Substring($name.indexof("<h1>")+4)
$Name = $name.Substring(0, $name.indexof("</h1>"))
$Name = $Name.Trim()
$Name = [System.Web.HttpUtility]::HtmlDecode($Name)

$Publisher = $r.RawContent.Substring($r.RawContent.indexof("<div
id=""title"" class=""intro"),2000)
$Publisher = $Publisher.Substring($Publisher.indexof("<h2>By")+7)
$Publisher = $Publisher.Substring(0, $Publisher.indexof("</h2>"))
$Publisher = $Publisher.Trim()
$Publisher = [System.Web.HttpUtility]::HtmlDecode($Publisher)

$Category = $r.RawContent.Substring($r.RawContent.indexof("Category:
"),2000)
$Category = $Category.substring($Category.IndexOf("?mt=8"">")+7)
$Category = $Category.substring(0, $Category.IndexOf("</a>"))
$Category = $Category.Trim()
$Category = [System.Web.HttpUtility]::HtmlDecode($Category)

$icon = $r.RawContent.Substring($r.RawContent.indexof(",itunes-
games"" parental-rating=""1"" class=""lookup product
application"">"),15000)
$icon = $icon.Substring($icon.indexof("<img")+4)
$icon = $icon.Substring($icon.indexof("src-swap-high-dpi="")+19)
$icon = $icon.Substring(0,$icon.indexof(""" src-load-auto-after-dom-
load"))
$icon = $icon.Trim()

$destination =
"$($env:windir)\temp\icon.$($icon.substring($icon.LastIndexOf(".")+1)
)"
Invoke-WebRequest $icon -OutFile $destination

$bmp = [System.Drawing.Image]::FromFile($destination)
$bmpResized = New-Object System.Drawing.Bitmap(250, 250)
$graph = [System.Drawing.Graphics]::FromImage($bmpResized)

$graph.Clear([System.Drawing.Color]::White)
$graph.DrawImage($bmp,0,0 , 250, 250)
$bmp.Dispose()
$bmpResized.Save($destination)
$bmpResized.Dispose()
```

Once this is done, if need, you create an application using the Get-CMApplication and New-CMApplication cmdlets. This is achieved by the following lines:

```
$App = Get-CMApplication -Name $AppName
if ($App -eq $null)
{
    $App = New-CMApplication -Name $AppName -AutoInstall $False -
IconLocationFile $destination -Publisher $Publisher -
LocalizedApplicationName $Name
}
```

After that, you create, if needed, a Deployment type iOS using the Get-CMDeploymentType and Add-CMDeploymentType cmdlets. This is achieved by the following lines:

```
$DT = Get-CMDeploymentType -ApplicationName $AppName | Where-Object {
$_.LocalizedDisplayName -eq "iOS" }
if ($dt -ne $null)
{
    continue
}
else
{
    Add-CMDeploymentType -ApplicationName
"$($app.LocalizedDisplayName)" -AutoIdentifyFromInstallationFile -
ForceForUnknownPublisher $True -InstallationFileLocation $url -
IosAppStoreInstaller -DeploymentTypeName iOS
}
```

Once done, you get the list of existing categories, querying the WMI class SMS_CategoryInstance and filter it when the CategoryTypeName property is equal to CatalogCategories. If the category does not exist, you create it using the New-CMCategory cmdlets. This is achieved by the following lines:

```
$CatalogcategoryList = gwmi -computername "$sdkserver" -Namespace
"root\sms\site_$SiteCode" -query "select * from SMS_CategoryInstance
where CategoryTypeName = 'CatalogCategories'"
$categoryList = $CatalogcategoryList | Where-Object
{$_.LocalizedCategoryInstanceName -eq $Category}
if ($categoryList -eq $nnull)
{
    New-CMCategory -Name $Category -CategoryType CatalogCategories |
out-null
}
```

Lastly, you assign the category to the application and remove the temporary icon using the Set-CMApplication and Remove-Item cmdlets. This is achieved by the following lines:

```
Set-CMApplication -Id "$($app.CI_ID)" -UserCategories $Category

Remove-Item $destination
```

And as a result, you would see all Applications created

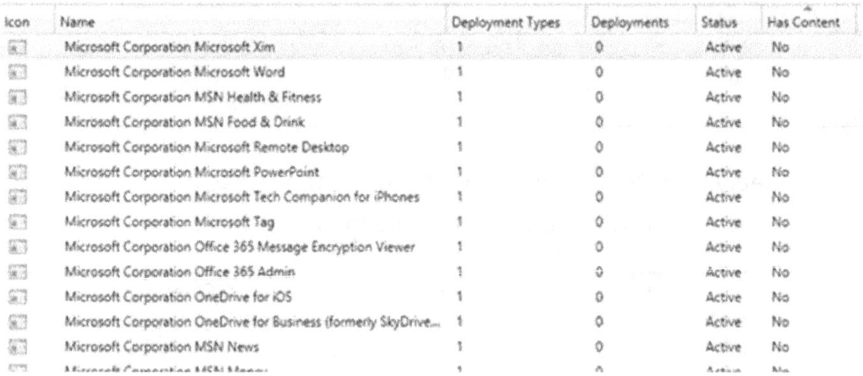

Icon	Name	Deployment Types	Deployments	Status	Has Content
	Microsoft Corporation Microsoft Xim	1	0	Active	No
	Microsoft Corporation Microsoft Word	1	0	Active	No
	Microsoft Corporation MSN Health & Fitness	1	0	Active	No
	Microsoft Corporation MSN Food & Drink	1	0	Active	No
	Microsoft Corporation Microsoft Remote Desktop	1	0	Active	No
	Microsoft Corporation Microsoft PowerPoint	1	0	Active	No
	Microsoft Corporation Microsoft Tech Companion for iPhones	1	0	Active	No
	Microsoft Corporation Microsoft Tag	1	0	Active	No
	Microsoft Corporation Office 365 Message Encryption Viewer	1	0	Active	No
	Microsoft Corporation Office 365 Admin	1	0	Active	No
	Microsoft Corporation OneDrive for iOS	1	0	Active	No
	Microsoft Corporation OneDrive for Business (formerly SkyDrive...	1	0	Active	No
	Microsoft Corporation MSN News	1	0	Active	No
	Microsoft Corporation MSN Money	1	0	Active	No

Figure 68. Part IV – Software Library - Script 02 (1)

Script 03

Scenario: You are a consultant and when you enable the software update point, you need to create Software Update Groups based on products, download the content from the internet for updates that apply to all languages or English and distribute it to a Distribution Point Group. You would like to create a single Deployment Group or multiple, based on the size of the environment, but would like to control it manually.

Note: All command lines and scripts used can be found on the `Part IV - Software Library - Script 03.ps1` PowerShell script file

First, you need to set some variables to be used during the script; these variables will hold the following:

- The Configuration Manager Site Code
- The SMS Provider server name
- Distribution Point group names
- path for the Software Update group
- Language of the updates to download (collation)
- Allow Software Update Group update if it already exist
- Allow creation of the Deployment Packages
- Allow creation of a single deployment package and if yes, its name
- Temporary folder location where the files are going to be downloaded

To achieve this, the script has the following lines:

```
$sitecode = 'CLC'
$sdkserver = 'SRV0007'
$DeploymentPackagePath = "\\server\share\softwareupdate"
$DistributionPointGroups = @("London")

$AllowUpdates = $true
$CreateDeploymentPackage = $true
$CreateSingleDeploymentPackage = $true
$SingleDeploymentGroupName = "All Updates"
$ContentLocales = "'Locale:0','Locale:9'"

$TempDownloadPath = "$($env:Temp)\$((Get-Date).Ticks)"
```

After this, you have some functions that you use. The first function is called `Get-Update`, used to download files from the internet using the .Net object `System.Net.WebClient` and saving it to a location in the hard drive that was passed as parameter. This is achieved by the following lines:

```
function Get-Update
{
    param (
        [string]$URL,
        [string]$Path
    )
    $File = Split-Path -Leaf $URL
    $FilePath = "$Path\$File"

    if (Test-Path $filePath) { return }

    try
    {
        $WebClient = New-Object System.Net.WebClient
        $WebClient.DownloadFile($URL, $FilePath)
    }
    catch
    {
        "Failed to download from [$URL]"
        "Error: $_"
    }
}
```

The second function is called `Create-CMDeploymentGroup`, used to create a Deployment Group. If it already exist, it will return the package ID. This is done by the `Get-CMSoftwareUpdateDeploymentPackage`. After this, you validate the existence of the Deployment Group and create the deployment group if it does not exist. This is achieved by the following lines:

```
function Create-CMDeploymentGroup
{
    param (
        [string]$Name,
        [string]$sdkserver,
        [string]$SiteCode,
        [string]$Path
    )

    $DeploymentGroup = Get-CMSoftwareUpdateDeploymentPackage -Name
"$Name"

    if ($DeploymentGroup -eq $null)
    {
        $class = [wmiclass]""
        $class.psbase.path =
"\\$($sdkserver)\root\sms\site_$($sitecode):SMS_SoftwareUpdatesPackag
e"
        $DeploymentGroup = $class.CreateInstance()
```

```
        $DeploymentGroup.Name = $Name
        $DeploymentGroup.SourceSite = $SiteCode
        $DeploymentGroup.PkgSourcePath = "$($Path)\$($Name)"
        $DeploymentGroup.PkgSourceFlag = [int32]2

        $DeploymentGroup.put() | out-null
        $DeploymentGroup.Get() | out-null
    }

    return $DeploymentGroup.PackageID
}
```

Note: The `Create-CMDeploymentGroup` function creates the Deployment Group using a WMI style as there is equivalent Configuration Manager cmdlet available yet.

The script actually starts here. First import the Configuration Manager PowerShell module if it does not exist for the Site Code and after that, you move to the Configuration Manager site. This is achieved by the following lines:

```
import-module
$env:SMS_ADMIN_UI_PATH.Replace("bin\i386","bin\ConfigurationManager.p
sd1") -force

if ((get-psdrive $SiteCode -erroraction SilentlyContinue |
measure).Count -ne 1)
{
    new-psdrive -Name $SiteCode -PSProvider
"AdminUI.PS.Provider\CMSite" -Root $sdkserver
}
cd "$($SiteCode):"
```

The next step is to validate if a single Deployment Group needs to be created and if yes, you create it. This is achieved by the following lines:

```
if (($CreateDeploymentPackage -eq $true) -and
($CreateSingleDeploymentPackage -eq $true))
{
    $pkgId = Create-CMDeploymentGroup -Name
"$SingleDeploymentGroupName" -sdkServer "$sdkserver" -SiteCode
"$SiteCode" -Path "$DeploymentPackagePath"
}
```

The next step is to get a list of all products that have been selected on the Software Update configuration. As you can see, this is done using a WMI query because it is easier than using the `Get-CMSoftwareUpdatePointComponent` and looking for the property `Props.SupportedUpdateLanguages`. This is achieved by the following lines:

```
$Products = gwmi -namespace "root\sms\site_$sitecode" -computername
$sdkserver -query "select LocalizedCategoryInstanceName,
CategoryInstance_UniqueID from SMS_UpdateCategoryInstance where
CategoryTypeName = 'Product' and AllowSubscription = 1 and
IsSubscribed = 1"
```

Now, for each product, you will get the name of the product, replace all dots (".") with none and add a Baseline to a product (i.e. "Baseline Office 2013" update group). This is achieved by the following lines:

```
$Name = $prod.LocalizedCategoryInstanceName
$Name = $Name.Replace(".","")
$BaselineName = "Baseline $Name"
```

Now, let's see if the baseline already exist using the Get-CMSoftwareUpdateGroup. If it exists and $AllowUpdates you will stop working with this product and move to the next one, otherwise, create the temporary directory to download the updates. This is achieved by the following lines:

```
$swUpdGroup = Get-CMSoftwareUpdateGroup -Name '$BaselineName'
if (($swUpdGroup -ne $null) -and ($AllowUpdates -eq $false)) {
continue }
New-Item -Path $TempDownloadPath -ItemType Directory | out-null
```

Now, it is time to get the list of updates that are applicable to the product with a WMI query. This is achieved by the following lines:

```
$updates = gwmi -namespace "root\sms\site_$sitecode" -computername
$sdkserver -Query "SELECT CI_ID FROM SMS_SoftwareUpdate where
IsExpired = 0 and IsSuperseded = 0 and CategoryInstance_UniqueIDs
like '%$($prod.CategoryInstance_UniqueID)%'"
```

After this, for each update, check the URL where the update can be downloaded from. Download only English and language agnostic updates, and ignore ia64 updates. This is achieved by the following lines:

```
$tmpCI_ID = 0
$updList = @()
$contentList = @()
$urlList = @()
$LocalSourcePath = @()
$updates | foreach {
    $tmpCI_ID = $_.CI_ID;
    gwmi -namespace "root\sms\site_$sitecode" -computername
$sdkserver -query "SELECT fil.* FROM SMS_CIToContent con,
SMS_CIContentFiles fil WHERE con.CI_ID='$($tmpCI_ID)' AND
```

```
con.ContentID=fil.ContentID and con.ContentLocales in
($ContentLocales)" |
    foreach {
        if ($_.SourceURL.Indexof("ia64") -lt 0)
        {
            $updList += $tmpCI_ID; $contentList += $_.ContentID;
$urlList += $_.SourceURL;
        }
    }
} | out-null
```

Then confirm that there is something to download and download it to the temporary location. This is achieved by the following lines:

```
if ($urllist.Count -lt 1) { continue }
$urllist | foreach { Get-Update -url $_ -Path $TempDownloadPath;
$LocalSourcePath += $TempDownloadPath }
```

Once all files have been downloaded, create the software update group if needed, otherwise, update the existing software update group. You can note that the creation of the update group was done by the New-CMSoftwareUpdateGroup while the update was done using the WMI Put() method of the WMI. This is because there is no other way to update an existing list of updates on a Software Update Group. This is achieved by the following lines:

```
if ($swUpdGroup -eq $null) { New-CMSoftwareUpdateGroup -Name
"$BaselineName" -UpdateId $updList | out-null }
else
{
    $swUpdGroup.Updates += $updList
    $swUpdGroup.Put() | out-null
}
```

Now, it is time to create the software update group. It will only be created if it is required. This is achieved by the following lines:

```
if (($CreateDeploymentPackage -eq $true) -and
($CreateSingleDeploymentPackage -eq $false))
{
    $pkgId = Create-CMDeploymentGroup -Name "$BaselineName" -sdkServer
"$sdkserver" -SiteCode "$SiteCode" -Path "$DeploymentPackagePath"
}
```

Now, confirm that the number of files that supposed to be download have been downloaded and if not, ignore adding the updates to the package. This is required because Configuration Manager needs to have the exactly the right number of updates. If the number of updates is not correct, the download is considered as failed. You will noticed that you are calling a WMI method `AddUpdateContent` of the `SMS_SoftwareUpdatesPackage` class as there is no other way to perform this action.

After that, distribute the content to all Distribution Point Groups using the `Start-CMContentDistribution` cmdlet and Remove the Temporary Files. This is achieved by the following lines:

```
if ($contentList.Count -ne $LocalSourcePath.Count) { continue }
else
{
    Invoke-WmiMethod -Path
"\\$($sdkserver)\root\sms\site_$($sitecode):SMS_SoftwareUpdatesPackag
e.PackageID='$pkgId'" -Name AddUpdateContent -ArgumentList
@($false,$contentList,$LocalSourcePath) | out-null
    if (($CreateDeploymentPackage -eq $true) -and
($CreateSingleDeploymentPackage -eq $false))
    {
        foreach ($dp in $DistributionPointGroups) { Start-
CMContentDistribution -DeploymentPackageId $pkgID -
DistributionPointGroupName $dp }
    }
}

Remove-Item $TempDownloadPath -Force -Recurse
```

Once it is done, perform the same actions for the next product and once there is no other product left, distribute the content to all distribution points, but this time only if you have created a single deployment package. This is achieved by the following lines:

```
if (($CreateDeploymentPackage -eq $true) -and
($CreateSingleDeploymentPackage -eq $true))
{
    foreach ($dp in $DistributionPointGroups) { Start-
CMContentDistribution -DeploymentPackageId $pkgID -
DistributionPointGroupName $dp }
}
```

And as a result, you would get all Software Update Groups created

Icon	Name	Description	Date Created	
	Baseline Adobe Systems - Adobe Reader XI		11/12/2014 16:58	
	Baseline CAPICOM		11/12/2014 13:27	
	Baseline Forefront Endpoint Protection 2010		11/12/2014 13:28	
	Baseline Forefront TMG		11/12/2014 13:28	
	Baseline Microsoft - System Center 2012 R2 Configuration Manager		11/12/2014 16:58	
	Baseline Microsoft SQL Server 2012		11/12/2014 14:57	
	Baseline Office 2013		11/12/2014 16:18	
	Baseline Report Viewer 2010		11/12/2014 13:29	
	Baseline SQL Server Feature Pack		11/12/2014 13:30	
	Baseline System Center 2012 R2 - Data Protection Manager		11/12/2014 16:27	
	Baseline System Center 2012 R2 - Virtual Machine Manager		11/12/2014 16:28	
	Baseline Visual Studio 2013		11/12/2014 16:28	
	Baseline Windows 7		11/12/2014 14:00	
	Baseline Windows 8		11/12/2014 14:18	
	Baseline Windows 81		11/12/2014 16:48	
	Baseline Windows Server 2008 R2		11/12/2014 14:38	
	Baseline Windows Server 2012 R2		11/12/2014 16:57	

Figure 69. Part IV – Software Library - Script 03 (1)

Script 04

Scenario: Every month, after the Patch Tuesday, you need to create a Software Update Group for all updates released that month. Download the content from the internet for updates that apply to all languages or English and distribute it to a Distribution Point Group. You would like to create a single Deployment Group or multiple, based on the size of the environment, but would like to control it manually.

Note: All command lines and scripts used can be found on the `Part IV - Software Library - Script 04.ps1` PowerShell script file

First, you need to set some variables to be used during the script; these variables will hold the following:

- The Configuration Manager Site Code
- The SMS Provider server name
- Distribution Point group names
- path for the Software Update group
- Language of the updates to download (collation)
- Allow Software Update Group update if it already exist
- Allow creation of the Deployment Packages
- Allow creation of a single deployment package and if yes, its name
- Temporary folder location where the files are going to be downloaded

To achieve this, the script has the following lines:

```
$sitecode = 'CLC'
$sdkserver = 'SRV0007'
$DeploymentPackagePath = "\\server\share\softwareupdate"
$DistributionPointGroups = @("London")

$AllowUpdates = $true
$CreateDeploymentPackage = $true
$CreateSingleDeploymentPackage = $true
$SingleDeploymentGroupName = "All Updates"
$ContentLocales = "'Locale:0','Locale:9'"

$TempDownloadPath = "$($env:Temp)\$((Get-Date).Ticks)"
```

After this, create a couple of functions. The first function is called `Get-Update`, used to download files from the internet using the .Net object `System.Net.WebClient` and saving it to a location in the hard drive that was passed as parameter. This is achieved by the following lines:

```
function Get-Update
{
    param (
        [string]$URL,
        [string]$Path
    )
    $File = Split-Path -Leaf $URL
    $FilePath = "$Path\$File"

    if (Test-Path $filePath) { return }

    try
    {
        $WebClient = New-Object System.Net.WebClient
        $WebClient.DownloadFile($URL, $FilePath)
    }
    catch
    {
        "Failed to download from [$URL]"
        "Error: $_"
    }
}
```

The second function is called Create-CMDeploymentGroup, used to create a Deployment Group. If it already exist, it will return the package ID. This is done by the Get-CMSoftwareUpdateDeploymentPackage. After this, you validate if the existence of the Deployment Group. Create the deployment group if it does not exist. This is achieved by the following lines:

```
function Create-CMDeploymentGroup
{
    param (
        [string]$Name,
        [string]$sdkserver,
        [string]$SiteCode,
        [string]$Path
    )

    $DeploymentGroup = Get-CMSoftwareUpdateDeploymentPackage -Name
"$Name"

    if ($DeploymentGroup -eq $null)
    {
        $class = [wmiclass]""
        $class.psbase.path =
"\\$($sdkserver)\root\sms\site_$($sitecode):SMS_SoftwareUpdatesPackag
e"
```

```
        $DeploymentGroup = $class.CreateInstance()

        $DeploymentGroup.Name = $Name
        $DeploymentGroup.SourceSite = $SiteCode
        $DeploymentGroup.PkgSourcePath = "$($Path)\$($Name)"
        $DeploymentGroup.PkgSourceFlag = [int32]2

        $DeploymentGroup.put() | out-null
        $DeploymentGroup.Get() | out-null
    }

    return $DeploymentGroup.PackageID
}
```

Note: The `Create-CMDeploymentGroup` function creates the Deployment Group using a WMI style as there is equivalent Configuration Manager cmdlet available yet.

The script actually starts here. First import the Configuration Manager PowerShell module if it does not exist for the Site Code and after that, you move to the Configuration Manager site. This is achieved by the following lines:

```
import-module
$env:SMS_ADMIN_UI_PATH.Replace("bin\i386","bin\ConfigurationManager.p
sdl") -force

if ((get-psdrive $SiteCode -erroraction SilentlyContinue |
measure).Count -ne 1)
{
    new-psdrive -Name $SiteCode -PSProvider
"AdminUI.PS.Provider\CMSite" -Root $sdkserver
}
cd "$($SiteCode):"
```

The next step is to validate the month and the date. Get all updates from the first day until the last day of the month. This is achieved by the following lines:

```
$NumberOfDays =
@("31","28","31","30","31","30","31","31","30","31","30","31")

$Today = Get-Date
$Month = $Today.Month
$Year = $Today.Year

$Begin = "$($Month)/01/$($Year)"
$End = "$($Month)/$($NumberOfDays[$Month-1])/$($Year)"
```

The next step is to validate if a single Deployment Group needs to be created and if yes, create it. This is achieved by the following lines:

```
if (($CreateDeploymentPackage -eq $true) -and
($CreateSingleDeploymentPackage -eq $true))
{
    $pkgId = Create-CMDeploymentGroup -Name
"$SingleDeploymentGroupName" -sdkServer "$sdkserver" -SiteCode
"$SiteCode" -Path "$DeploymentPackagePath"
}
```

Then name the update group as Year-Month (i.e. 2014-November) so it will be easy to see which updates were released that month. This is achieved by the following lines:

```
$Name = "$($Year)-$($Month)"
```

Now, let's see if the baseline already exist using the Get-CMSoftwareUpdateGroup. If it exist and $AllowUpdates is true, stop working with this product and move to the next one, otherwise, create the temporary directory to where the updates will be downloaded. This is achieved by the following lines:

```
$swUpdGroup = Get-CMSoftwareUpdateGroup -Name '$Name'
if (($swUpdGroup -ne $null) -and ($AllowUpdates -eq $false)) {
continue }
New-Item -Path $TempDownloadPath -ItemType Directory | out-null
```

Now, it is time to get the list of updates that are have been released that month by querying the WMI class SMS_SoftwareUpdate and filtering it by the Date the update was released. This is achieved by the following lines:

```
$Updates = gwmi -namespace "root\sms\site_$sitecode" -computername
$sdkserver -Query "SELECT ci.CI_ID FROM SMS_SoftwareUpdate ci  WHERE
(DatePosted >='$($Begin) 00:00:00' AND DatePosted <='$($End)
23:59:00' ) AND (IsExpired ='0' ) AND (IsSuperseded ='0' ) AND (
CI_ID not in (select CI_ID from SMS_CIAllCategories where
CategoryInstance_UniqueID = 'UpdateClassification:e0789628-ce08-4437-
be74-2495b842f43b') ) AND ( CI_ID not in (select CI_ID from
SMS_CIAllCategories where CategoryInstance_UniqueID =
'Product:a38c835c-2950-4e87-86cc-6911a52c34a3') ) ORDER BY
DateRevised DESC"
```

After this, for each update, check the URL where the update can be downloaded from. Download only English and language agnostic updates, and ignore ia64 updates. This is achieved by the following lines:

```
$tmpCI_ID = 0
$updList = @()
$contentList = @()
$urlList = @()
$LocalSourcePath = @()
$updates | foreach {
    $tmpCI_ID = $_.CI_ID;
    gwmi -namespace "root\sms\site_$sitecode" -computername
$sdkserver -query "SELECT fil.* FROM SMS_CIToContent con,
SMS_CIContentFiles fil WHERE con.CI_ID='$($tmpCI_ID)' AND
con.ContentID=fil.ContentID and con.ContentLocales in
($ContentLocales)" |
    foreach {
        if ($_.SourceURL.Indexof("ia64") -lt 0)
        {
            $updList += $tmpCI_ID; $contentList += $_.ContentID;
$urlList += $_.SourceURL;
        }
    }
} | out-null
```

Confirm that there is something to download and download it to the temporary location. This is achieved by the following lines:

```
if ($urllist.Count -lt 1) { continue }
$urllist | foreach { Get-Update -url $_ -Path $TempDownloadPath;
$LocalSourcePath += $TempDownloadPath }
```

Once all files have been downloaded, create the software update group if necessary. Otherwise, update the existing software update group. You can note that the creation of the update group was done by the New-CMSoftwareUpdateGroup while the update was done using the WMI Put() method of the WMI. This is because there is no other way to update an existing list of updates on a Software Update Group. This is achieved by the following lines:

```
if ($swUpdGroup -eq $null) { New-CMSoftwareUpdateGroup -Name
"$BaselineName" -UpdateId $updList | out-null }
else
{
    $swUpdGroup.Updates += $updList
    $swUpdGroup.Put() | out-null
}
```

Now, it is time to create the software update group. It will only be created if it is required. This is achieved by the following lines:

```
if (($CreateDeploymentPackage -eq $true) -and
($CreateSingleDeploymentPackage -eq $false))
{
    $pkgId = Create-CMDeploymentGroup -Name "$BaselineName" -sdkServer
"$sdkserver" -SiteCode "$SiteCode" -Path "$DeploymentPackagePath"
}
```

Now, confirm that the number of files that supposed to be download have been downloaded and if not, ignore adding the updates to the package. This is required because Configuration Manager needs to have the exactly the right number of updates. If the number of updates is not correct, the download is considered as failed. You will noticed that you are calling a WMI method AddUpdateContent of the SMS_SoftwareUpdatesPackage class as there is no other way to perform this action.

After that, distribute the content to all Distribution Point Groups using the Start-CMContentDistribution cmdlet and remove the temporary files. This is achieved by the following lines:

```
if ($contentList.Count -ne $LocalSourcePath.Count) { continue }
else
{
    Invoke-WmiMethod -Path
"\\$($sdkserver)\root\sms\site_$($sitecode):SMS_SoftwareUpdatesPackag
e.PackageID='$pkgId'" -Name AddUpdateContent -ArgumentList
@($false,$contentList,$LocalSourcePath) | out-null
    foreach ($dp in $DistributionPointGroups)
    {
        Start-CMContentDistribution -DeploymentPackageId $pkgID -
DistributionPointGroupName $dp
    }
}

Remove-Item $TempDownloadPath -Force -Recurse
```

And as a result, you would get all Software Update Groups created

Icon	Name		Description	Date Created	Last Date Modified
	2014-12			16/12/2014 18:29	16/12/2014 18:29

Figure 70. Part IV – Software Library - Script 04 (1)

Script 05

Scenario: You are a consultant and you need to create a Package to update the Anti-Virus signature on all machines with the latest version.

Note: All command lines and scripts used can be found on the `Part IV - Software Library - Script 05.ps1` PowerShell script file

First, you need to set some variables to be used during the script; these variables will hold the following:

- The Configuration Manager Site Code
- The SMS Provider server name
- Distribution Point group names
- Package information (Name, Version, Manufacturer, Language and Path)
- Program Information (Name and command line)

To achieve this, the script has the following lines:

```
$SiteCode = "CLC"
$SDKServer = "SRV0007"
$DPGroupName = "Headquarters"

$PackageName = "McAfee AV Signature Update"
$PackageVersion = ""
$PackageManufacturer = "McAfee"
$PackageLanguage = "English"
$PackagePath = "\\server\share"

$ProgramName = "Install Latest AV Signature"
$ProgramCommandLine = "InstallSignature.exe"
```

Next, import the Configuration Manager PowerShell module if it does not exist for the Site Code and after that, you move to the Configuration Manager site. This is achieved by the following lines:

```
import-module
$env:SMS_ADMIN_UI_PATH.Replace("bin\i386","bin\ConfigurationManager.p
sd1") -force

if ((get-psdrive $SiteCode -erroraction SilentlyContinue |
measure).Count -ne 1)
{
    new-psdrive -Name $SiteCode -PSProvider
"AdminUI.PS.Provider\CMSite" -Root $sdkserver
}
cd "$($SiteCode):"
```

After this, create the Package if it does not exist. Use the Get-CMPackage and New-CMPackage cmdlets. Once the package is created, set the priority and the update schedule, as you always want the Distribution Point to have the latest AV signature update. Use the Set-CMPackage cmdlet to set the priority, but to set the schedule, you need to use WMI function as there is no cmdlet available. This is achieved by the following lines:

```
$CMPackage = Get-CMPackage -Name "$PackageName"
if ($CMPackage -eq $null)
{
    $CMPackage = New-CMPackage -Name "$PackageName" -Language
"$PackageLanguage" -Manufacturer "$PackageManufacturer" -Version
"$PackageVersion" -Path "$PackagePath"
    Set-CMPackage -Name "$PackageName " -DistributionPriority High

    $WMIclass = [wmiclass]""
    $WMIClass.psbase.Path =
"\\$($sdkserver)\root\sms\site_$($sitecode):SMS_ST_RecurInterval"
    $UpdateSchedule = $WMIClass.CreateInstance()
    $UpdateSchedule.DayDuration = 0
    $UpdateSchedule.DaySpan = 1
    $UpdateSchedule.HourDuration = 0
    $UpdateSchedule.HourSpan = 0
    $UpdateSchedule.IsGMT = $false
    $UpdateSchedule.MinuteDuration = 0
    $UpdateSchedule.MinuteSpan = 0
    $UpdateSchedule.StartTime = "20150101000000.000000+***"

    $WMIPkg =
[wmi]"\\$($sdkserver)\root\sms\site_$($sitecode):SMS_Package.PackageI
D='$($CMPackage.PackageID)'"
    $WMIPkg.RefreshSchedule = $UpdateSchedule
    $WMIPkg.Put() | out-null
}
```

Now, create the program if it does not exist with the Get-CMProgram and New-CMProgram cmdlet. After that, you need to set some properties for the program that you cannot be set when creating it. To set the properties use the Set-CMProgram cmdlet. This is achieved by the following lines:

```
$CMProgram = Get-CMProgram -ProgramName "$ProgramName" -PackageId
$CMPackage.PackageID
if ($CMProgram -eq $null)
{
    $CMProgram = New-CMProgram -CommandLine $ProgramCommandLine -
PackageName "$PackageName" -StandardProgramName "$ProgramName" -
DriveMode RenameWithUnc -ProgramRunType WhetherOrNotUserIsLoggedOn -
RunMode RunWithAdministrativeRights -RunType Hidden -UserInteraction
$False
    Set-CMProgram -Name "$PackageName" -ProgramName "$ProgramName" -
StandardProgram -AfterRunningType NoActionRequired -
EnableTaskSequence $True -SuppressProgramNotifications $True -
UserInteraction $False
}
```

Once done, distribute the content to a Distribution Point group and deploy the package to a collection, to run every day at 10:00. This is achieved by the following lines:

```
Start-CMContentDistribution -DistributionPointGroupName "$DPGroup" -
PackageID "$($CMPackage.PackageID)"

$DeploySchedule = New-CMSchedule -RecurInterval Days -RecurCount 1 -
Start "01/01/2015 10:00:00"
Start-CMPackageDeployment -CollectionName "All Desktop and Server
Clients" -PackageName "$PackageName" -ProgramName "$ProgramName" -
StandardProgram -AllowUsersRunIndependently $False -DeployPurpose
Required -FastNetworkOption
DownloadContentFromDistributionPointAndRunLocally -RerunBehavior
AlwaysRetunProgram -Schedule $DeploySchedule -SendWakeUpPacket $True
-SlowNetworkOption DownloadContentFromDistributionPointAndLocally -
SoftwareInstallation $True -SystemRestart $False -UseMeteredNetwork
$True -UseUtcForAvailableSchedule $False -UseUtcForExpireSchedule
$False
```

And as a result, you would have the package created and deployed to our collection

Figure 71. Part IV – Software Library - Script 05 (1)

Part V – Administration

The Administration allows you to learn cmdlets that will enable management of a Configuration Manager 2012 R2 environment. In this part, you will provide some scripts to allow automation of some of the day-to-day tasks required for a Configuration Manager Administrator or Consultant.

The following sections have a selection of scripts that have proven to save time and automation day-to-day tasks in a Configuration Manager environment.

Script 01

Scenario: You are a consultant and need to split the packages and applications into folders where each folder represent the current development cycle (i.e. Dev, UAT and Prod). The folders already exist and there are packages and applications into each folder. You need to automate the creation of the Security Scope and assign it the correct security scope to the applications and packages in the specific folder.

Note: All command lines and scripts used can be found on the Part V – Administration – Script 01.ps1 PowerShell script file

First, you need to set some variables to be used during the script; these variables will hold the following:

- The Configuration Manager Site Code
- The SMS Provider server name
- Authorized Security Scopes, scopes that will not be removed
- List of valid security scopes, that will be created if do not exist

To achieve this, the script has the following lines:

```
$sdkServer = "srv0007.corp.local"
$sitecode = "clc"
$authorizedSecScope = @("OSD", "Default")
$secscopeList = @("UAT", "DEV", "PROD")
```

Next, import the Configuration Manager PowerShell module if it does not exist for the Site Code and after that, you move to the Configuration Manager site. This is achieved by the following lines:

```
import-module
$env:SMS_ADMIN_UI_PATH.Replace("bin\i386","bin\ConfigurationManager.p
sd1") -force

if ((get-psdrive $SiteCode -erroraction SilentlyContinue |
measure).Count -ne 1)
{
    new-psdrive -Name $SiteCode -PSProvider
"AdminUI.PS.Provider\CMSite" -Root $sdkserver
}
cd "$($SiteCode):"
```

The next part of the script will run for each Security Scope and if they do not exist, it will be created. You will be using Get-CMSecurityScope and New-CMSecurityScope cmdlets. This is achieved by the following lines:

```
foreach ($secScope in $secscopeList)
{
    if ((get-cmSecurityScope -name $secScope) -eq $null)
    {
        New-CMSecurityScope -name $secScope
    }
}
```

Once you have the security scopes created, query for all package and application folders that have the name as the security scope (based on the $secscopeList variable). This is achieved by the following lines:

```
$ContainerList = gwmi -computername "$sdkserver" -Namespace
"root\sms\site_$SiteCode" -query "select * from
SMS_ObjectContainerNode where ObjectTypeName in
('SMS_Package','SMS_ApplicationLatest') and Name in ('$($secscopeList
-join("' , '"))')"
```

Now it is where the fun begins, for each folder get the Security Scope assigned to it (by the name using the Get-CMSecurityScope). This is achieved by the following lines:

```
$SecurityScope = get-cmSecurityScope -name ($container.name)
```

Once you have the security scope, collect the list of packages or applications that are located in the folder. Because you are looking for different classes (packages and applications), you have two different queries for it, depending on the $container.ObjectTypeName. This is achieved by the following lines:

For applications, querying the WMI class SMS_ApplicationLatest:

```
$AppList = gwmi -computername "$sdkserver" -Namespace
"root\sms\site_$SiteCode" -query "SELECT App.* FROM
SMS_ApplicationLatest app, SMS_ObjectContainerItem ci WHERE
app.ModelName = ci.InstanceKey and ci.ContainerNodeID =
$($container.ContainerNodeID) and app.IsHidden=0"
```

For Packages, querying the WMI class SMS_Package:

```
$PackageList = gwmi -computername "$sdkserver" -Namespace
"root\sms\site_$SiteCode" -query "SELECT pkg.* FROM SMS_Package pkg,
SMS_ObjectContainerItem ci WHERE pkg.PackageID = ci.InstanceKey and
ci.ContainerNodeID = $($container.ContainerNodeID) and
pkg.ActionInProgress!=3 AND pkg.PackageType = 0"
```

For each application or package, get the list of current assigned security scope and if the security scope does not have the right security scope yet, assign it. This can be achieved by the following lines:

For Applications using the Set-CMApplication cmdlet:

```
$SecurityScopes = $App.SecuredScopeNames
if ($container.Name -notin $SecurityScopes)
{
    Set-CMApplication -SecurityScopeName ($container.Name) -Name
$App.LocalizedDisplayName -SecurityScopeAction AddMembership | out-
null
}
```

For Packages, using the method AddMemberships of the WMI Class SMS_SecuredCategoryMembership:

```
$SecurityScopes = $pkg.SecuredScopeNames
if ($container.Name -notin $SecurityScopes)
{
    Invoke-WmiMethod -computername "$sdkserver" -Namespace
"Root\SMS\Site_$SiteCode" -Name AddMemberShips -Class
SMS_SecuredCategoryMemberShip -ArgumentList
$SecurityScope.CategoryID,$pkg.PackageID,2 | out-null
}
```

Lastly, remove all security scopes that should not be there (i.e. You moved an application from the DEV folder to the UAT folder, so the DEV security scope should be removed). This is achieved by the following lines:

For Applications using the Set-CMApplication cmdlet:

```
foreach ($SScope in $SecurityScopes)
{
    if ($Sscope -in $authorizedSecScope) { continue }
    if ($SScope.ToLower() -eq $container.name) { continue }

    Set-CMApplication -SecurityScopeName $SScope -Name
$App.LocalizedDisplayName -SecurityScopeAction RemoveMembership |
out-null
}
```

For Packages, using the method RemoveMemberShips of the WMI Class SMS_SecuredCategoryMemberShip:

```
foreach ($SScope in $SecurityScopes)
{
    if ($Sscope -in $authorizedSecScope) { continue }
    if ($SScope.ToLower() -eq $container.name) { continue }
    $SecScope = gwmi -computername "$sdkserver" -Namespace
"root\sms\site_$SiteCode" -query "SELECT * FROM SMS_SecuredCategory
where CategoryName = '$SScope'"

    Invoke-WmiMethod -computername "$sdkserver" -Namespace
"Root\SMS\Site_$SiteCode" -Name RemoveMemberShips -Class
SMS_SecuredCategoryMemberShip -ArgumentList
$SecScope.CategoryID,$pkg.PackageID,2 | out-null
}
```

As you can see, there are already cmdlets to manage the application security scope, but not for packages. This is the reason that you need to use WMI commands.

And as a result, you would get all Applications and Packages with the Correct Security Scope for the folder

Icon	Name	Deployment Types	Deployments	Status	Security Scopes
	VideoLAN VLC media player 2.1.5	1	0	Active	"UAT", "Default"
	Microsoft Office Professional Plus 2013	2	0	Active	"UAT", "Default"

Figure 72. Part V – Administration - Script 01 (1)

Script 02

Scenario: You are a consultant and you need to create a new client settings for cloud distribution point and another for companywide device settings.

Note: All command lines and scripts used can be found on the `Part V – Administration – Script 02.ps1` PowerShell script file

First, you need to set some variables to be used during the script; these variables will hold the following:

- The Configuration Manager Site Code
- The SMS Provider server name
- Company Name
- Remote Viewers Group Name
- Cloud Distribution Point collection name
- Client Settings Companywide Name

To achieve this, the script has the following lines:

```
$SiteCode = "CLC"
$SDKServer = "SRV0007"
$CompanyName = "RFL Systems"
$RemoteViewers = "CORP\SCCM Remote Viewers"
$CollName = "Allow Cloud DP"
$ClientSettingsName = "CompanyWide Client Settings"
```

Next, import the Configuration Manager PowerShell module if it does not exist for the Site Code and after that, you move to the Configuration Manager site. This is achieved by the following lines:

```
import-module
$env:SMS_ADMIN_UI_PATH.Replace("bin\i386","bin\ConfigurationManager.p
sd1") -force

if ((get-psdrive $SiteCode -erroraction SilentlyContinue |
measure).Count -ne 1)
{
    new-psdrive -Name $SiteCode -PSProvider
"AdminUI.PS.Provider\CMSite" -Root $sdkserver
}
cd "$($SiteCode):"
```

The next part of the script will actually create a new Client Settings, it is done by the `New-CMClientSetting` cmdlet. This is achieved by the following lines:

```
New-CMClientSetting -Name "$ClientSettingsName" -Type Device
New-CMClientSetting -Name "Allow Cloud Distribution Point" -Type
Device
```

Once you have created the client settings, it is time to set the client settings properties, it is done by the Set-CMClientSetting cmdlet. The script will enable the Cloud Services Settings for the Allow Cloud DP client settings and set the following properties for the Companywide settings:

- Computer Agent Settings
  - Organization Name is set
  - Install permissions to All Users
  - Suspend Bitlocker Pin set to Never
  - PowerShell execution policy set to Bypass
- Computer Restart Settings
  - Display temporary notification set to 1440
  - Display final countdown set to 45
- Software Inventory
  - Enable is set to No
- Remote Tools Settings
  - Enabled and Firewall exception set to Domain
  - Users can change policy set to NO
  - Allow Remote Control of unattended computer set to YES
  - Prompt for users permission set to YES
  - Grant Remote Control to Local Administrators set to YES
  - Access allowed set to Full Control
  - Set the Remote Viewers
  - Show session notification icon on taskbar set to YES
  - Play sound set to No Sound
  - Manage unsolicited and solicited Remote Assistance Settings set to YES
  - Level of remote assistance set to NONE
  - Manage Remote Desktop settings and allow permitted viewers to connect using RDP set to YES
  - Require network level authentication set to No
- User Device Affinity Settings
  - User define usage threshold (minutes) set to 2800
  - User define usage threshold (days) set to 20
  - Automatically configure user device affinity from usage data set to YES

This is achieved by the following lines:

```
Set-CMClientSetting -ComputerAgentSettings -Name
"$ClientSettingsName" -BrandingTitle $CompanyName -InstallRestriction
AllUsers -PowerShellExecutionPolicy Bypass -SuspendBitLocker Never
Set-CMClientSetting -ComputerRestartSettings -Name
"$ClientSettingsName" -
RebootLogoffNotificationCountdownDurationMinutes 1440 -
RebootLogoffNotificationFinalWindowMinutes 45
Set-CMClientSetting -SoftwareInventorySettings -Name
"$ClientSettingsName" -EnableSoftwareInventory $False
Set-CMClientSetting -UserDeviceAffinitySettings -Name
"$ClientSettingsName" -AllowUserAffinity $True -AutoApproveAffinity
$True -UserAffinityLogOnThresholdMinutes 2800 -
UserAffinityUsageThresholdDays 20
Set-CMClientSetting -RemoteToolsSettings -Name "$ClientSettingsName"
-AccessLevel FullControl -AllowClientChange $False -
AllowPermittedViewersToRemoteDesktop $True -
AllowRemoteControlOfUnattendedComputer $True -AudibleSignal
PlayNoSound -FirewallExceptionProfile Domain -
GrantRemoteControlPermissionToLocalAdministrator $True -
ManageRemoteDesktopSetting $True -ManageSolicitedRemoteAssistance
$True -ManageUnsolicitedRemoteAssistance $True -
PromptUserForPermission $True -RemoteAssistanceAccessLevel None -
RequireAuthentication $False -ShowNotificationIconOnTaskbar $True -
ShowSessionConnectionBar $True -PermittedViewer "$RemoteViewers"
Set-CMClientSetting -CloudServicesSettings -Name "Allow Cloud
Distribution Point" -AllowCloudDistributionPoint $True
```

Then it is time to create the collection that will allow cloud distribution point access if it does not exist. To do this, use the `Get-CMDeviceCollection` cmdlet to check if the collection already exists and `New-CMDeviceCollection` cmdlet to create a new collection if needed. This is achieved by the following lines:

```
$coll = Get-CMDeviceCollection -Name "$CollName"
if ($coll -eq $null)
{
    New-CMDeviceCollection -LimitingCollectionName "All Desktop and
Server Clients" -Name "$CollName"
}
```

Finally, deploy the client settings to the correct collections with the `Start-CMClientSettingDeployment` cmdlet. This is achieved by the following lines:

```
Start-CMClientSettingDeployment -ClientSettingName
$ClientSettingsName -CollectionName "All Desktop and Server Clients"
Start-CMClientSettingDeployment -ClientSettingName
$ClientSettingsName -CollectionName "$CollName"
```

As a result, you would see all necessary custom client settings deployed to the right collections.

Figure 73. Part V – Administration - Script 02 (1)

Script 03

Scenario: You are a consultant and when you install a new remote distribution point, you also need to add to a distribution point group (create it if needed) and distribute the content to the distribution point group.

Note: All command lines and scripts used can be found on the `Part V – Administration – Script 03.ps1` PowerShell script file

First, you need to set some variables to be used during the script; these variables will hold the following:

- The Configuration Manager Site Code
- The SMS Provider server name
- New distribution point server name (FQDN)
- Distribution Point Group name

To achieve this, the script has the following lines:

```
$SiteCode = "CLC"
$SDKServer = "SRV0007"
$NewServer = "srv0016.corp.local"
$DPGroupName = "Headquarters"
```

Next, import the Configuration Manager PowerShell module if it does not exist for the Site Code and after that, you move to the Configuration Manager site. This is achieved by the following lines:

```
import-module
$env:SMS_ADMIN_UI_PATH.Replace("bin\i386","bin\ConfigurationManager.p
sdl") -force

if ((get-psdrive $SiteCode -erroraction SilentlyContinue |
measure).Count -ne 1)
{
    new-psdrive -Name $SiteCode -PSProvider
"AdminUI.PS.Provider\CMSite" -Root $sdkserver
}
cd "$($SiteCode):"
```

The next part of the script will actually install the Distribution Point with the `New-CMSiteSystemServer` and `Add-CMDistributionPoint` cmdlets. This is achieved by the following lines:

```
New-CMSiteSystemServer -SiteCode $SiteCode -UseSiteServerAccount -
ServerName $newServer
Add-CMDistributionPoint -CertificateExpirationTimeUtc "$((Get-
Date).AddYears(20).ToString())" -SiteSystemServerName $newServer -
SiteCode $siteCode -MinimumFreeSpaceMB 50 -EnablePXESupport -
AllowRespondIncomingPxeRequest -EnableUnknownComputerSupport -
EnableValidateContent
```

Once you have initiated the installation of the new distribution point, create a Distribution Point Group only if it does not exist and add the new distribution point to the distribution point group. You will be using the Get-CMDistributionPointGroup and New-CMDistributionPointGroup cmdlets. This is achieved by the following lines:

```
$DPGroup = Get-CMDistributionPointGroup -Name $DPGroupName
if ($DPGroup -eq $null)
{
    New-CMDistributionPointGroup -name $DPGroupName
}
Add-CMDistributionPointToGroup -DistributionPointName $NewServer -
DistributionPointGroupName $DPGroupName
```

Then it is time to distribute the content to the new created distribution point group. To do this, use the Start-CMContentDistribution cmdlet. This cmdlet allows you to specify the content type, based on specific variables (i.e. if you use PackageID, you need to use a Package while if you use ApplicationName you need to use an Application). As you need to distribute all the existing content to the new distribution point group, query the object and for each instance of the object you distribute it to the distribution point group. This is achieved by the following lines:

```
Get-CMPackage | where-object { $_.PkgSourcePath -ne "" } | foreach {
Start-CMContentDistribution -DistributionPointGroupName $DPGroupName
-PackageID $_.PackageID }
Get-CMApplication | foreach { Start-CMContentDistribution -
DistributionPointGroupName $DPGroupName -ApplicationName
"$($_.LocalizedDisplayName)" }
Get-CMSoftwareUpdateDeploymentPackage | foreach { Start-
CMContentDistribution -DistributionPointGroupName $DPGroupName -
DeploymentPackageId $_.PackageID }
Get-CMBootImage | foreach { Start-CMContentDistribution -
DistributionPointGroupName $DPGroupName -BootImageId $_.PackageID }
Get-CMDriverPackage | foreach { Start-CMContentDistribution -
DistributionPointGroupName $DPGroupName -DriverPackageName
"$($_.Name)" }
Get-CMOperatingSystemImage | foreach { Start-CMContentDistribution -
DistributionPointGroupName $DPGroupName -OperatingSystemImageId
$_.PackageID }
Get-CMTaskSequence | foreach { Start-CMContentDistribution -
DistributionPointGroupName $DPGroupName -TaskSequenceId $_.PackageID
}
```

And as a result, all necessary packages are distributed to the distribution point group.

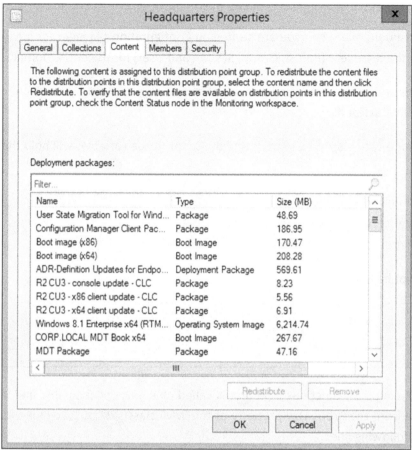

Figure 74. Part V – Administration - Script 03 (1)

Script 04

Scenario: You are a consultant and when you are setting up Configuration Manager for small companies, you enable the discovery (Forest, Group, System and User) for the entire domain.

Note: All command lines and scripts used can be found on the Part V - Administration - Script 04.ps1 PowerShell script file

First, you need to set some variables to be used during the script; these variables will hold the following:

- The Configuration Manager Site Code
- The SMS Provider server name, FQDN format
- Domain Information

To achieve this, the script has the following lines:

```
$SiteCode = "CLC"
$SDKServer = "SRV0007.CORP.LOCAL"
$domainName = "LDAP://DC=$($env:USERDNSDOMAIN.Split(".") -join
",DC=")"
```

After this, you create a couple of functions. The first is called ChangePropComponent and is used to change a value from the Props lazy property of the WMI class SMS_SCI_Component. This is achieved by the following lines:

```
Function ChangePropComponent
{
    PARAM(
        $sdkServer,
        $siteCode,
        $property,
        $value,
        $value1,
        $value2,
        $componentname,
        $addvalue1 = $false,
        $increasebyvalue = $false
    )

    $component = gwmi -Namespace ("root\sms\site_$siteCode") -
ComputerName ($sdkServer) -query ('select * from SMS_SCI_Component
where FileType=2 and ItemName = "' + $componentname + '" and
ItemType="Component" and SiteCode="' + $siteCode + '"')
    $props = $component.Props
    $prop = $props | where {$_.PropertyName -eq $property}

    if ($value -ne $null)
    {
        if ($increasebyvalue -eq $true) { $prop.Value = [int]$value +
[int]$prop.Value }
        else { $prop.Value = $value }
    }

    if ($value1 -ne $null)
    {
        if ($addvalue1)
        { $prop.Value1 += $value1 }
        else
        { $prop.Value1 = $value1 }
    }

    if ($value2 -ne $null)
    {
        $prop.Value2 = $value2
    }

    $component.Props = $props
    $component.Put() | Out-Null
}
```

Another function used is called ChangeComponent that is used to change a property for the component of the WMI class SMS_SCI_Component. This is achieved by the following lines:

```
Function ChangeComponent
{
    PARAM(
        $sdkServer,
        $siteCode,
        $property,
        $value,
        $componentname
    )

    $component = gwmi -Namespace ("root\sms\site_$siteCode") -
ComputerName ($sdkServer) -query ('select * from SMS_SCI_Component
where FileType=2 and ItemName = "' + $componentname + '" and
ItemType="Component" and SiteCode="' + $siteCode + '"')
    $Component.$property = $value
    $component.Put() | Out-Null
}
```

Another function used is called `ChangePropListComponent` that is used to change a property of a component that exists under the propList lazy property. This is achieved by the following lines:

```
Function ChangePropListComponent
{
    PARAM(
        $sdkServer,
        $siteCode,
        $property,
        $value,
        $componentname
    )

    $component = gwmi -Namespace ("root\sms\site_$siteCode") -
ComputerName ($sdkServer) -query ('select * from SMS_SCI_Component
where FileType=2 and ItemName = "' + $componentname + '" and
ItemType="Component" and SiteCode="' + $siteCode + '"')
    $propLists = $component.PropLists
    $propLists = $propLists | where {$_.PropertyName -eq $property}
    if ($propLists -ne $null)
    {
        $propLists.Values = $value
        $component.PropList = $propLisst
    }
    else
    {
        $Component.PropLists +=
[System.Management.ManagementBaseObject](Set-WMIPropertyList -
sdkserver $sdkserver -sitecode $sitecode -PropertyName $property -
Values $value)
    }
    $component.Put() | Out-Null
}
```

The last function called Set-WMIPropertyList is used by the ChangePropListComponent to
add a new property to the propList lazy property. This is achieved by the following lines:

```
Function Set-WMIPropertyList
{
    PARAM(
        $sdkserver,
        $SiteCode,
        $PropertyName,
        [array]$Values
    )

    $embeddedpropertylist_class = [wmiclass]""
    $embeddedpropertylist_class.psbase.Path = "\\" + $sdkserver +
"\ROOT\SMS\site_" + $SiteCode + ":SMS_EmbeddedPropertyList"
    $embeddedpropertylist =
$embeddedpropertylist_class.createInstance()

    $embeddedpropertylist.PropertyListName = $PropertyName
    $embeddedpropertylist.Values = $Values

    return $embeddedpropertylist
}
```

Once you have the functions, it is time to change the properties for the discovery. For all discovery methods, there are 4 mains areas:

- Component Name
- Properties Configuration
- Enable discovery
- Force discovery to run

The Component Name is set by the variable $DiscoveryComponent and can have the one of the following values:

- SMS_AD_FOREST_DISCOVERY_MANAGER used for Forest Discovery
- SMS_AD_SYSTEM_DISCOVERY_AGENT used for System Discovery
- SMS_AD_USER_DISCOVERY_AGENT used for User Discovery
- SMS_AD_SECURITY_GROUP_DISCOVERY_AGENT used for Group Discovery

Once you have the discovery variable set, you can set the properties. Each discovery has its own properties that is changed using one of the functions created before.

For the forest discovery, use the following lines:

```
ChangePropComponent -sdkServer $sdkServer -sitecode $siteCode -
property 'Enable AD Site Boundary Creation' -value 1 -componentname
("$($DiscoveryComponent)|$($sdkserver)")
ChangePropComponent -sdkServer $sdkServer -sitecode $siteCode -
property 'Enable Subnet Boundary Creation' -value 1 -componentname
("$($DiscoveryComponent)|$($sdkserver)")
```

For the System Discovery, use the following lines:

```
ChangePropListComponent -sdkServer $sdkServer -sitecode $siteCode -
property 'AD Containers' -value (@($domainName,'0','1')) -
componentname ("$($DiscoveryComponent)|$($sdkserver)")
ChangePropComponent -sdkServer $sdkServer -sitecode $siteCode -
property 'Enable Filtering Expired Logon' -value 1 -componentname
("$($DiscoveryComponent)|$($sdkserver)")
ChangePropComponent -sdkServer $sdkServer -sitecode $siteCode -
property 'Enable Filtering Expired Password' -value 1 -componentname
("$($DiscoveryComponent)|$($sdkserver)")
```

For the User Discovery, use the following lines:

```
ChangePropListComponent -sdkServer $sdkServer -sitecode $siteCode -
property 'AD Containers' -value (@($domainName,'0','1')) -
componentname ("$($DiscoveryComponent)|$($sdkserver)")
```

For the Group Discovery, use the following lines:

```
ChangePropListComponent -sdkServer $sdkServer -sitecode $siteCode -
property ('Search Bases:domain '+($env:USERDNSDOMAIN)) -value
(@($domainName)) -componentname
("$($DiscoveryComponent)|$($sdkserver)")
ChangePropListComponent -sdkServer $sdkServer -sitecode $siteCode -
property 'AD Containers' -value (@('domain
'+($env:USERDNSDOMAIN)),'0','0','1') -componentname
("$($DiscoveryComponent)|$($sdkserver)")
ChangePropComponent -sdkServer $sdkServer -sitecode $siteCode -
property 'Enable Filtering Expired Logon' -value 1 -componentname
("$($DiscoveryComponent)|$($sdkserver)")
ChangePropComponent -sdkServer $sdkServer -sitecode $siteCode -
property 'Enable Filtering Expired Password' -value 1 -componentname
("$($DiscoveryComponent)|$($sdkserver)")
```

Once the setting has been changed, enable the discovery to run. This can be accomplished by the following line:

```
ChangePropComponent -sdkServer $sdkServer -sitecode $siteCode -
property 'SETTINGS' -value 0 -value1 'ACTIVE' -componentname
("$($DiscoveryComponent)|$($sdkserver)")
```

Lastly, run the discovery and increase (or set) the `Run Count`. This is achieved by the following lines:

```
ChangePropComponent -sdkServer $sdkServer -sitecode $siteCode -
property 'Run Count' -value 1 -componentname
("$($DiscoveryComponent)|$($sdkserver)") -increasebyvalue $true
ChangeComponent -sdkServer $sdkServer -sitecode $siteCode -property
'Flag' -value 6 -componentname
("$($DiscoveryComponent)|$($sdkserver)")
```

And as a result, you have enabled the discovery methods and configured to perform the discovery for the whole domain

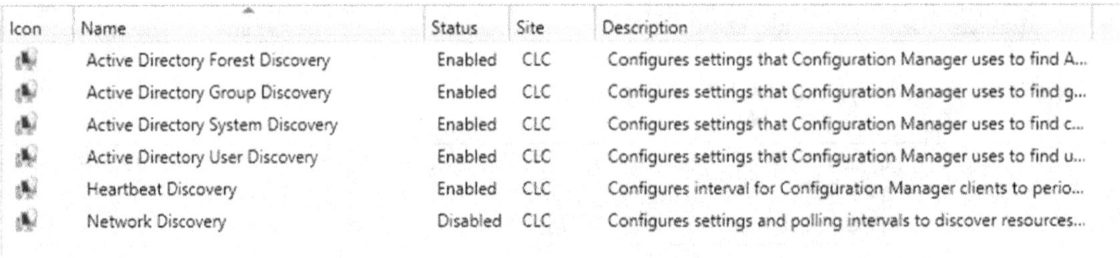
Icon
Name
Status
Site
Description
Active Directory Forest Discovery
Enabled
CLC
Configures settings that Configuration Manager uses to find A...
Active Directory Group Discovery
Enabled
CLC
Configures settings that Configuration Manager uses to find g...
Active Directory System Discovery
Enabled
CLC
Configures settings that Configuration Manager uses to find c...
Active Directory User Discovery
Enabled
CLC
Configures settings that Configuration Manager uses to find u...
Heartbeat Discovery
Enabled
CLC
Configures interval for Configuration Manager clients to perio...
Network Discovery
Disabled
CLC
Configures settings and polling intervals to discover resources...

Figure 75. Part V – Administration - Script 04 (1)

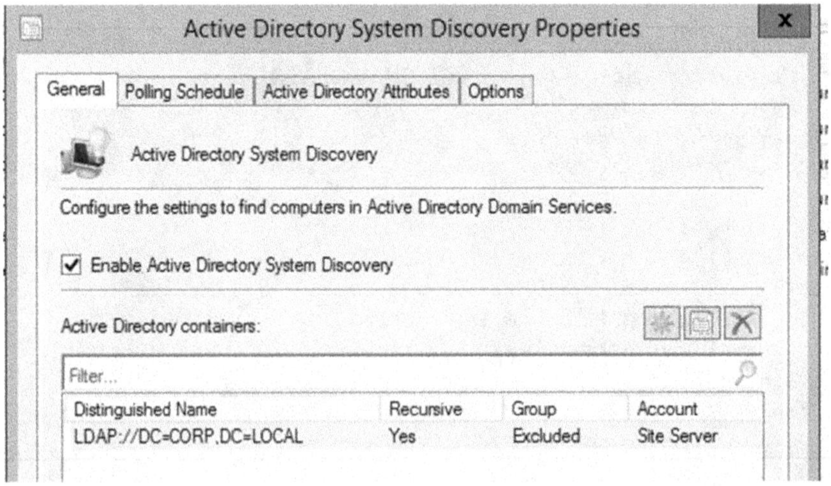
Active Directory System Discovery Properties
General
Polling Schedule
Active Directory Attributes
Options
Active Directory System Discovery
Configure the settings to find computers in Active Directory Domain Services.
Enable Active Directory System Discovery
Active Directory containers:
Filter...
Distinguished Name
Recursive
Group
Account
LDAP://DC=CORP,DC=LOCAL
Yes
Excluded
Site Server

Figure 76. Part V – Administration - Script 04 (2)

Script 05

Scenario: You are a consultant and want to create a boundary group based on the Active Directory sites after you have enabled and run the forest discovery. The boundary group should have the Active Directory Site boundary as well as any IP address range boundaries created for the Active Directory site boundary.

Note: All command lines and scripts used can be found on the Part V - Administration - Script 05.ps1 PowerShell script file

First, you need to set some variables to be used during the script; these variables will hold the following:

- The Configuration Manager Site Code
- The SMS Provider server name

To achieve this, the script has the following lines:

```
$SiteCode = "CLC"
$SDKServer = "SRV0007.CORP.LOCAL"
```

Next, import the Configuration Manager PowerShell module if it does not exist for the Site Code and after that, you move to the Configuration Manager site. This is achieved by the following lines:

```
import-module
$env:SMS_ADMIN_UI_PATH.Replace("bin\i386","bin\ConfigurationManager.p
sd1") -force

if ((get-psdrive $SiteCode -erroraction SilentlyContinue |
measure).Count -ne 1)
{
    new-psdrive -Name $SiteCode -PSProvider
"AdminUI.PS.Provider\CMSite" -Root $sdkserver
}
cd "$($SiteCode):"
```

The next part of the script will actually get the information of all Active Directory Boundaries that have been created. To do this, use the Get-CMBoundary cmdlet and filter for the BoundaryType is equal to 1 (Boundary type indicates how Configuration Manager identify the boundary. Possible values are IPSUBNET (0), ADSITE (1), IPV6PREFIX (2) and IPRANGE (3).). The command will return only Active Directory Site boundary type. This is achieved by the following lines:

```
$BoundaryList = $Boundaries = Get-CMBoundary | Where-Object
{$_.BoundaryType -eq 1 }
```

Once you have the list of Active Directory Site boundaries, create the boundary group for each boundary if it does not exist. For this, use the Get-CMBoundaryGroup and New-CMBoundaryGroup cmdlets. This is achieved by the following lines:

```
$BoundaryGroup = Get-CMBoundaryGroup -Name "$Name"
if ($BoundaryGroup -eq $null)
{
    $BoundaryGroup = New-CMBoundaryGroup -Name "$Name"
}
```

Next step search for all related boundaries, including any IP Range boundaries with the Get-CMBoundary cmdlet, but this time filter by the boundary name. This is achieved by the following lines:

```
$AllRelatedBoundaries = Get-CMBoundary -BoundaryName "*$($Name)*"
```

Once you have the list of related boundaries, add it to the Boundary Group using the Add-CMBoundaryToGroup cmdlet. This is achieved by the following lines:

```
$AllRelatedBoundaries | Add-CMBoundaryToGroup -BoundaryGroupName
"$Name"
```

And as a result, you will get the boundary groups created.

Icon	Name	Member Count
	Brazil	2
	HongKong	2
	London	2
	Rome	2
	Singapore	2

Figure 77. Part V – Administration - Script 05 (1)

Part VI – Console Extension

Configuration Manager console uses a XML-based architecture that can easily be extended. The XML defines how the Configuration Manager console looks and behaves.

When creating console extensions for Configuration Manager there are several components to consider:

- Console Extension Type: many different types of extensions are supported, including: Actions, Forms, Views, Nodes, and Management Classes.
- Console Component GUID: this GUID corresponds to the console component on which the custom action will be added.
- Extension Folder: Each custom extension will be created and placed in a specific location for console consumption. This location will vary depending on what type of console extension is being created
- XML File: each console extension has its own custom XML file.

As everything is based on XML file, it is necessary to render the Configuration Manager console hierarchy, the results pane, and the action pane. The following table shows the folder structure and its usage:

Folder	Description
ConsoleRoot	This folder contains various XML files that define built in user interface elements and classes. • ManagementClassDescriptions.xml: definitions for the SMS Provider classes. • ConnectedConsole.xml: definitions for sticky nodes and go-to navigation. • AssetManagementNode.xml, MonitoringNode.xml, SiteConfigurationNode.xml, SoftwareLibraryNode.xml: definitions for each workspace in the Configuration Manager console.
Extensions	Location for XML that is related to the SMS Provider. There are four types of extension folders: • Actions. XML files for Configuration Manager console actions. • Forms. XML files for form extensions to the Configuration Manager console. • Nodes. XML files for node extensions to the Configuration Manager console. • Management Classes. XML files for management class extensions to the Configuration Manager console.
Other	Various helper XML files.
Validation	Validation rules for the Configuration Manager console forms.

Table 2. Part VI – Console Extension Folder description

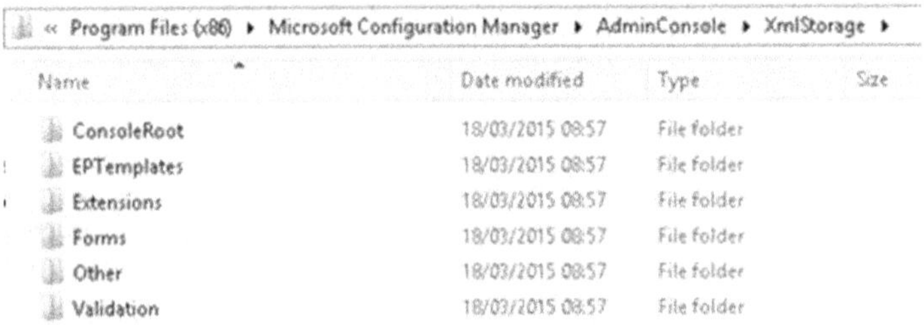

Figure 78. Part VI – Console Extension (1)

When you deploy a Configuration Manager extension, you install the files in the following directories:

Extension Type	Directory
Actions	<AdminConsole Installation Dir>\bin for the assembly <AdminConsole Installation Dir>\XmlStorage\Extensions\Actions for the action XML files
Forms	<AdminConsole Installation Dir>\bin for the assembly <AdminConsole Installation Dir>\XmlStorage\Extensions\Forms for the action XML files
Views	<AdminConsole Installation Dir>\bin for the assembly
Nodes	<AdminConsole Installation Dir>\bin for the assembly <AdminConsole Installation Dir>\XmlStorage\Extensions\Nodes for the action XML files
ManagementClasses	<AdminConsole Installation Dir>\bin for the assembly <AdminConsole Installation Dir>\XmlStorage\Extensions\ManagementClasses for the action XML files

Table 3. Part VI – Console Extension – Extension Type and Folder Location

Note: Not every extension is necessary to have an assembly. As example of Action execution, most of the time you will not need an assembly file, but if you want to add a custom image, this image will be added to a resource assembly. Another example if for forms, where you will be creating the form using some tools (i.e. Visual Studio) and the compiled project will generate a DLL that will be added to the assembly folder.

Now, let's look how to extend the console, adding new Executable Actions, but before you can determine the location in which to place your custom extension XML file, you will need to find the GUID corresponding to the console component on which you would like our custom action to be added. In other words if you want to add our action to the Assets and Compliance / Devices section of the console, you need to determine the specific GUID for the location. In order to identify these GUID's you must traverse existing root console XML files and manually (or using a script) locate these GUID's.

Unfortunately there are multiple files corresponding to the multiple Configuration Manager nodes and these files are located under <AdminConsole Installation Dir>\XmlStorage\ConsoleRoot.

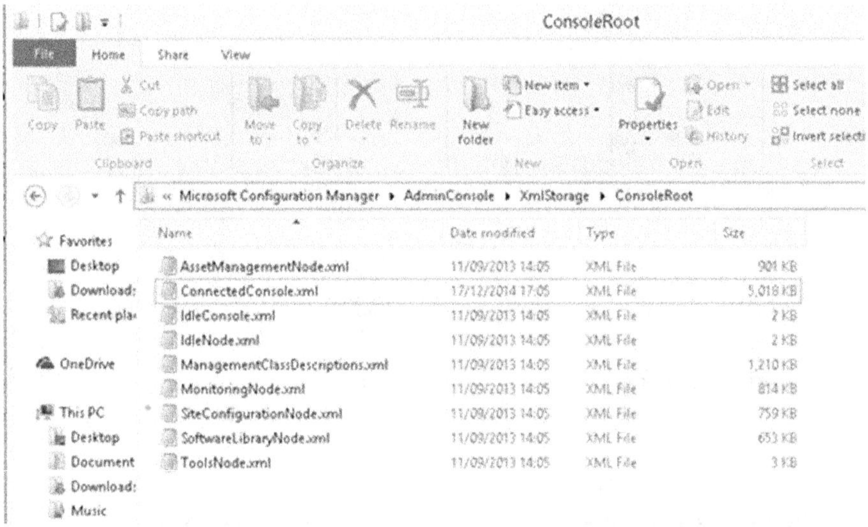

Figure 79. Part VI – Console Extension (2)

Fortunately, Configuration Manager gives us a tool called AdminUI.ConsoleBuilder.exe that is found under <AdminConsole Installation Dir>\Bin. Once you open, you need open the ConnectedConsole to be able to see anything.

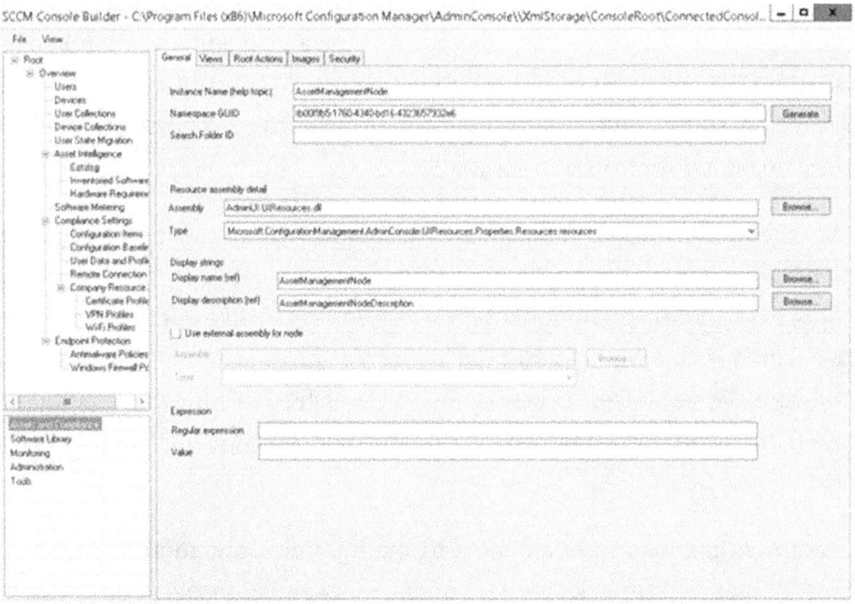

Figure 80. Part VI – Console Extension (3)

What the AdminUI.ConsoleBuilder.exe does is to open the ConnectedConsole.xml file under <AdminConsole Installation Dir>\XmlStorage\ConsoleRoot. What about the other files?

You could open each one manually and get the GUID's, but if you want to automate the discovery, you can use the following PowerShell script, that will create a folder and a file under <AdminConsole Installation Dir>\XmlStorage\Actions.

```
$XMLFiles = Get-ChildItem
$env:SMS_ADMIN_UI_PATH.Replace("bin\i386","XmlStorage\ConsoleRoot") -
Include *.xml -Recurse
$Folder =
$env:SMS_ADMIN_UI_PATH.Replace("bin\i386","XmlStorage\Extensions\Acti
ons")
foreach ($file in $XMLFiles)
{
    $Content = gc $file
    foreach ($line in  ($Content | Select-String -Pattern
"NamespaceGUID="))
    {
        $arrNamespace = $line.ToString() -Split("NameSpaceGUID=")
        $ConsoleGUID = ($arrNamespace[1] -split '"')[1]
        New-Item -Path $Folder -Name $ConsoleGUID -ItemType Directory
-Force
@"
<ActionDescription Class="Group" DisplayName="$($ConsoleGUID)"
MnemonicDisplayName="Test"
Description="Test"><ShowOn><string>DefaultHomeTab</string><string>Con
textMenu</string>  </ShowOn><ActionGroups> <ActionDescription
Class="Executable" DisplayName="Test1" MnemonicDisplayName="Test1"
Description = "Test1"
RibbonDisplayType="TextAndSmallImage"><ShowOn><string>ContextMenu</st
ring><string>DefaultHomeTab</string></ShowOn><Executable><FilePath>te
st.exe</FilePath><Parameters></Parameters></Executable></ActionDescri
ption></ActionGroups></ActionDescription>
"@ | Out-File -FilePath "$($Folder)\$($ConsoleGUID)\1.XML" -Force
    }
}
```

As a result, the next time you open the Console, you would see a new group under the Ribbon and a new context menu:

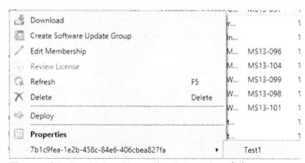

Figure 81. Part VI – Console Extension (4)

Now that you know where to add your XML file, how do you create one? It is simple: each file has many attributes and elements that are based on the action you want.

If you want to create an Executable Action, the first set of elements and attributes needed are for the Group Class. This will allow you to set the group (or submenu) name and if it should be a group in the Ribbon.

The following elements and attributes will be used:

- ActionDescription: group description displayed in the context menu or ribbon
- DisplayName: group name displayed in the context menu or ribbon
- MnemonicDisplayName: The mnemonic display name (mnemonic is intended to assist help memorize the name).
- GroupAsRegion: Boolean attribute specifies whether or not to display this group as a region on the ribbon bar
- ShowOn: Where this group should appear? This should contain a string for ribbon with DefaultHomeTab and / or context menu with ContextMenu

The result should be similar to:

```
<ActionDescription Class="Group" GroupAsRegion="false"
DisplayName="RFL Systems" MnemonicDisplayName="RFL Systems"
Description="RFL Systems custom Actions">
    <ShowOn>
        <string>DefaultHomeTab</string>
        <string>ContextMenu</string>
    </ShowOn>
```

The next part is for the Group Actions. It has only one element called ActionGroups. This is because it will have one or more sub-elements that will define the items that will appear in the Ribbon or submenu. For each action, you need to define the basic information as:

- ActionDescription: Action description displayed in the context menu or ribbon
- DisplayName: Action name displayed in the context menu or ribbon
- MnemonicDisplayName: The mnemonic display name.
- RibbonDisplayType: Define ribbon display rules

The result should be similar to:

```
<ActionGroups>
    <ActionDescription Class="Executable" DisplayName="Superseded by"
MnemonicDisplayName="Superseded by" Description = "Superseded by"
RibbonDisplayType="TextAndSmallImage">
```

For each action, you also need to define where they will appear, using the ShowOn option, as explained before. The result should be similar to:

```
<ShowOn>
    <string>DefaultHomeTab</string>
    <string>ContextMenu</string>
</ShowOn>
```

You now need to use the ImagesDescription, that is the information about the action's icon. This element requires the following information:

- Assembly: A resource DLL that exists under <AdminConsole Installation Dir>\bin
- Type: the resource type
- ImageResourceName: The name of the image

The result should be similar to:

```
<ImagesDescription>
    <ResourceAssembly>
        <Assembly>AdminUI.CollectionProperty.dll</Assembly>
<Type>Microsoft.ConfigurationManagement.AdminConsole.CollectionProper
ty.Properties.Resources.resources</Type>
    </ResourceAssembly>
    <ImageResourceName>Collection</ImageResourceName>
</ImagesDescription>
```

Lastly, you need to use the Executable element, which is the most important because it defines the executable file and parameters for the application. This element requires the following information:

- FilePath: Specify a location of the executable file
- Parameters: Parameters that will be passed to the executable file

The result should be similar to:

```
<Executable>
    <FilePath>PowerShell.exe</FilePath>
    <Parameters>-ExecutionPolicy bypass -File
c:\Scripts\CM12R2Console\CollectionPerComputer.ps1</Parameters>
</Executable>
```

How can you pass parameters like the Resource ID, Collection ID, etc? It is simple: Configuration Manager accept dynamic parameters starting with "##SUB:". This instructs Configuration Manager to use the current WMI object information.

The result should be similar to:

```
<Executable>
    <FilePath>PowerShell.exe</FilePath>
    <Parameters>-ExecutionPolicy bypass -File
c:\Scripts\CM12R2Console\CollectionPerComputer.ps1 "##SUB:__Server##"
"##SUB:__Namespace##" "##SUB:ResourceID##"</Parameters>
</Executable>
```

Where can you find which parameter you can use? Those are defined in the object class. If you are looking for a Device, the class would be SMS_R_Resource and using PowerShell, you can find all possible Properties:

```
gwmi -Namespace root\sms\site_clc -class sms_r_system | Get-Member |
Where-Object {$_.MemberType -eq "Property"}
```

The result should be similar to:

Figure 82. Part VI – Console Extension (5)

Now, putting our XML together, you would have:

```xml
<ActionDescription Class="Group" GroupAsRegion="false"
DisplayName="RFL Systems" MnemonicDisplayName="RFL Systems"
Description="RFL Systems custom Actions">
    <ShowOn>
        <string>DefaultHomeTab</string>
        <string>ContextMenu</string>
    </ShowOn>
    <ActionGroups>
        <ActionDescription Class="Executable" DisplayName="List all
Collections" MnemonicDisplayName="List all Collections" Description =
"List all Collections" RibbonDisplayType="TextAndSmallImage">
            <ShowOn>
            <string>DefaultHomeTab</string>
            <string>ContextMenu</string>
            </ShowOn>
            <ImagesDescription>
                <ResourceAssembly>

<Assembly>AdminUI.CollectionProperty.dll</Assembly>

<Type>Microsoft.ConfigurationManagement.AdminConsole.CollectionProper
ty.Properties.Resources.resources</Type>
                </ResourceAssembly>
                <ImageResourceName>Collection</ImageResourceName>
            </ImagesDescription>
            <Executable>
                <FilePath>PowerShell.exe</FilePath>
                <Parameters>-ExecutionPolicy bypass -File
c:\Scripts\CM12R2Console\CollectionPerComputer.ps1 "##SUB:__Server##"
"##SUB:__Namespace##" "##SUB:ResourceID##"</Parameters>
            </Executable>
        </ActionDescription>
    </ActionGroups>
</ActionDescription>
```

And as a result, you would see the new Group being created under the Devices as well as a context menu.

Figure 83. Part VI – Console Extension (6)

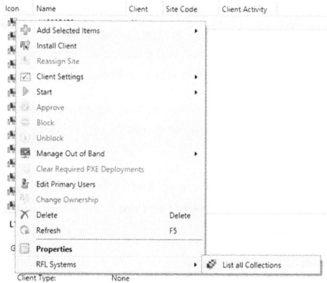

Figure 84. Part VI – Console Extension (7)

Part VII – Extras

The Extras section of the book allows you to learn more about the Configuration Manager automation. In this section, you will find few extra scripts that will help you with some of the day-to-day tasks required for a Configuration Manager Administrator or Consultant.

The following sections have a selection of scripts that have proven to save time and automation day-to-day tasks in a Configuration Manager environment.

Script 01

Scenario: You are a consultant and you are asked to create folders for Packages and Applications based on the Manufacturer property of the object and move the object to the correct folder.

Note: All command lines and scripts used can be found on the `Part VI – Extras - Script 01.ps1` PowerShell script file

First, you need to set some variables to be used during the script; these variables will hold the following:

- The Configuration Manager Site Code
- The SMS Provider server name

To achieve this, the script has the following lines:

```
$SiteCode = "CLC"
$SDKServer = "SRV0007"
```

Next, import the Configuration Manager PowerShell module if it does not exist for the Site Code and after that, you move to the Configuration Manager site. This is achieved by the following lines:

```
import-module
$env:SMS_ADMIN_UI_PATH.Replace("bin\i386","bin\ConfigurationManager.p
sd1") -force

if ((get-psdrive $SiteCode -erroraction SilentlyContinue |
measure).Count -ne 1)
{
    new-psdrive -Name $SiteCode -PSProvider
"AdminUI.PS.Provider\CMSite" -Root $sdkserver
}
cd "$($SiteCode):"
```

The next part of the script is specific for Applications. It will query all applications that are hosted on the Root folder. It means that any application that is already inside a folder will be ignored. Query the WMI by the SMS_ApplicationLatest and SMS_ObjectContainerItem classes. This is achieved by the following lines:

```
$AppList = gwmi -computername "$sdkserver" -Namespace
"root\sms\site_$SiteCode" -query "select App.* from
SMS_ApplicationLatest app where app.ModelName not in (select
InstanceKey from SMS_ObjectContainerItem where ObjectTypeName in
('SMS_ApplicationLatest'))"
```

Once you have a list of all applications, get the name of the Manufacturer, create a folder (if it does not exist) and move the Application to it. Because there is no built-in cmdlets, you need to use WMI. For applications, query the WMI class SMS_ApplicationLatest and SMS_ObjectContainerNode and create a folder if needed. Create a new instance of the class SMS_ObjectContainerNode with the Set-WMIInstance using the correct parameters. Once you have the folder, move it using the MoveMembers method of the SMS_objectContainerItem WMI class. This is achieved by the following lines:

```
$FolderName = $App.Manufacturer

$ContainerList = gwmi -computername "$sdkserver" -Namespace
"root\sms\site_$SiteCode" -query "select * from
SMS_ObjectContainerNode where ObjectTypeName in
('SMS_ApplicationLatest') and Name = '$FolderName'"

if ($ContainerList -eq $null)
{
    $Arguments = @{Name = "$FolderName"; ObjectType = 6000;
ParentContainerNodeId = 0}
    $newFolder = Set-WmiInstance -computername $sdkserver -Namespace
"root\sms\site_$sitecode" -Class "SMS_ObjectContainerNode" -Arguments
$Arguments
    $ContainerID = $newFolder.ContainerNodeID
}
else { $ContainerID = $ContainerList.ContainerNodeID }

[Array]$AppModelNameList = $App.ModelName
$TargetFolderID = $ContainerID
$RootFolderID = 0
$ObjectTypeID = 6000

Invoke-WmiMethod -computername $sdkserver -Namespace
"root\sms\site_$sitecode" -Class SMS_objectContainerItem -Name
MoveMembers -ArgumentList
$RootFolderID,$AppModelNameList,$ObjectTypeID,$TargetFolderID
```

After all applications are moved to the correct folder, it is time to get the list of all packages that are in the root of the package folder. Because there is no built-in cmdlets, you need to use WMI. Now query the WMI class SMS_Package and SMS_ObjectContainerItem. This is achieved by the following lines:

```
$PkgList = gwmi -computername "$sdkserver" -Namespace
"root\sms\site_$SiteCode" -query "select pkg.* from SMS_Package pkg
where pkg.PackageID not in (select InstanceKey from
SMS_ObjectContainerItem where ObjectTypeName in ('SMS_Package'))"
```

Once you have a list of all packages, get the name of the Manufacturer, create a folder (if it does not exist) and move the Package. Because there is no built-in cmdlets, use WMI. Query the WMI class SMS_Package and SMS_ObjectContainerNode and create a folder if needed. A new instance of the class SMS_ObjectContainerNode with the Set-WMIInstance using the correct parameters. Once you have the folder, move it using the MoveMembers method of the SMS_objectContainerItem WMI class. This is achieved by the following lines:

```
$FolderName = $Pkg.Manufacturer

$ContainerList = gwmi -computername "$sdkserver" -Namespace
"root\sms\site_$SiteCode" -query "select * from
SMS_ObjectContainerNode where ObjectTypeName in ('SMS_Package') and
Name = '$FolderName'"

if ($ContainerList -eq $null)
{
    $Arguments = @{Name = "$FolderName"; ObjectType = 2;
ParentContainerNodeId = 0}
    $newFolder = Set-WmiInstance -computername $sdkserver -Namespace
"root\sms\site_$sitecode" -Class "SMS_ObjectContainerNode" -Arguments
$Arguments
    $ContainerID = $newFolder.ContainerNodeID
}
else { $ContainerID = $ContainerList.ContainerNodeID }

[Array]$AppModelNameList = $pkg.PackageID
$TargetFolderID = $ContainerID
$RootFolderID = 0
$ObjectTypeID = 2

Invoke-WmiMethod -computername $sdkserver -Namespace
"root\sms\site_$sitecode" -Class SMS_objectContainerItem -Name
MoveMembers -ArgumentList
$RootFolderID,$AppModelNameList,$ObjectTypeID,$TargetFolderID
```

And as a result, you would see all necessary folders created and the applications / packages being moved to the folder

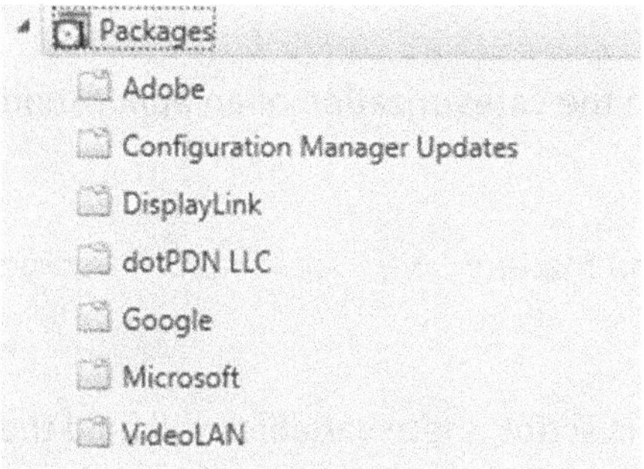

Figure 85. Part VII – Extras - Script 01 (1)

Script 02

Scenario: You are a consultant and you are asked to keep the categorization of an application as per asset intelligence.

Note: All command lines and scripts used can be found on the Part VI – Extras – Script 02.ps1 PowerShell script file

First, you need to set some variables to be used during the script; these variables will hold the following:

- The Configuration Manager Site Code
- The SMS Provider server name

To achieve this, the script has the following lines:

```
$SiteCode = "CLC"
$SDKServer = "SRV0007"
```

Next, import the Configuration Manager PowerShell module if it does not exist for the Site Code and after that, you move to the Configuration Manager site. This is achieved by the following lines:

```
import-module
$env:SMS_ADMIN_UI_PATH.Replace("bin\i386","bin\ConfigurationManager.p
sd1") -force

if ((get-psdrive $SiteCode -erroraction SilentlyContinue |
measure).Count -ne 1)
{
    new-psdrive -Name $SiteCode -PSProvider
"AdminUI.PS.Provider\CMSite" -Root $sdkserver
}
cd "$($SiteCode):"
```

Now you need to get the list of applications and the list of the existing user category. You do it using the Get-CMApplication cmdlets and querying the WMI class SMS_CategoryInstance. This is achieved by the following lines:

```
$applist = Get-CMApplication | where-object {$_.IsExpired -eq $false}
$CatalogcategoryList = gwmi -computername "$sdkserver" -Namespace
"root\sms\site_$SiteCode" -query "select * from SMS_CategoryInstance
where CategoryTypeName = 'CatalogCategories'"
```

Once you have the list of applications, you need to validate the user category for each application. The user category is not one of the default properties, instead, it is written on the `AppMgmtDigest.Application.DisplayInfo.info.UserCategories.Tag` (this is the Application Catalog User categories) when you read the XML. To be able to read the XML, you need to extract the `SDMPackageXML`. This is achieved by the following lines:

```
$xml = [xml]$app.SDMPackageXML
$displayInfoList = $xml.AppMgmtDigest.Application.DisplayInfo
$userCategoryList =
$xml.AppMgmtDigest.Application.DisplayInfo.info.UserCategories.Tag
$userCategoryNames = @()
```

Once you have the information that you want, populate an array with all current user categories. This will later on be used to update the user category list. This is achieved by the following lines:

```
foreach ($userCategory in $userCategoryList)
{
    $categoryList = $CatalogcategoryList | Where-Object
{$_.CategoryInstance_UniqueID -eq $userCategory}
    if ($CategoryList -ne $null)
    {
        foreach ($Category in $CategoryList)
        { $userCategoryNames +=
$Category.LocalizedCategoryInstanceName }
    }
}
$categoryName = $userCategoryNames
```

Then it is time to check to see if Configuration Manager has any information, in the asset intelligence database, for the application. Look at each node under the `AppMgmtDigest.Application.DisplayInfo` and for each `Info.Title` (this is the Application Catalog Localized application name), check the database. This is achieved by the following lines:

```
$swlist = gwmi -computername "$sdkserver" -Namespace
"root\sms\site_$SiteCode" -query "select * from SMS_AISoftwareList
where CommonName like '%$($displayInfo.Info.Title)%' and
OfficialCategoryName <> 'Unidentified'"
```

For each software title found, check if the category is official, it means that only categories set by Microsoft will be considered. This is achieved by the following lines:

```
if ($categoryName.IndexOf($sw.OfficialCategoryName) -ge 0) { continue
}
```

The next step is to check if the category already exist in the user category database and if it does not exist, create it with the New-CMCategory cmdlet. Once created, add it to the array of the user category. This is achieved by the following lines:

```
$categoryList = $CatalogcategoryList | Where-Object
{$_.LocalizedCategoryInstanceName -eq $sw.OfficialCategoryName}
if ($categoryList -eq $nnull)
{
    New-CMCategory -Name $sw.OfficialCategoryName -CategoryType
CatalogCategories | out-null

    $CatalogcategoryList = gwmi -computername "$sdkserver" -Namespace
"root\sms\site_$SiteCode" -query "select * from SMS_CategoryInstance
where CategoryTypeName = 'CatalogCategories'"
}
$categoryName += $sw.OfficialCategoryName
```

Lastly, you need to update the application with the new category list. Use the cmdlet Set-CMApplication and it was achieved by the following lines:

```
Set-CMApplication -Name $app.LocalizedDisplayName -UserCategories
$categoryName
```

And as a result, you would see all necessary user category being added

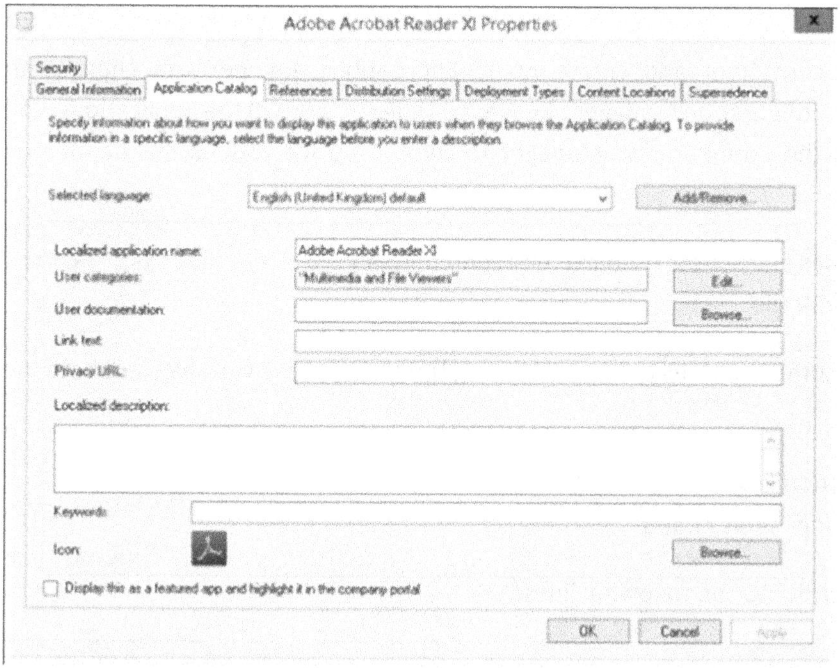

Figure 86. Part VII – Extras - Script 02 (1)

Script 03

Scenario: You are a consultant and create many applications and perform changes to applications, causing Configuration Manager to have multiple revisions of the applications. You do not want to leave the Configuration Manager to clean it up for you, as this happen by default every 60 days.

Note: All command lines and scripts used can be found on the Part VI – Extras – Script 03.ps1 PowerShell script file

First, you need to set some variables to be used during the script; these variables will hold the following:

- The Configuration Manager Site Code
- The SMS Provider server name

To achieve this, the script has the following lines:

```
$SiteCode = "CLC"
$SDKServer = "SRV0007"
```

Next, import the Configuration Manager PowerShell module if it does not exist for the Site Code and after that, you move to the Configuration Manager site. This is achieved by the following lines:

```
import-module
$env:SMS_ADMIN_UI_PATH.Replace("bin\i386","bin\ConfigurationManager.psd1") -force

if ((get-psdrive $SiteCode -erroraction SilentlyContinue | measure).Count -ne 1)
{
    new-psdrive -Name $SiteCode -PSProvider
"AdminUI.PS.Provider\CMSite" -Root $sdkserver
}
cd "$($SiteCode):"
```

Now you need to get the list of applications on your environment using the Get-CMApplication cmdlets. This is achieved by the following lines:

```
$cmApps = Get-CMApplication
```

Once you have the list of applications, you need to, for each application, get the list of the revisions with the Get-CMApplicationRevisionHistory cmdlet. This is achieved by the following lines:

```
$cmAppRevision = $cmApp | Get-CMApplicationRevisionHistory
```

Then delete all old revisions using the Remove-CMApplicationRevisionHistory cmdlets. This is achieved by the following lines:

```
for ($i = 0;$i -lt $cmAppRevision.Count-1;$i++)
{
     Remove-CMApplicationRevisionHistory -ID $cmApp.CI_ID -revision
$cmAppRevision[$i].CIVersion -force
}
```

And as a result, you would see all necessary revision being removed.

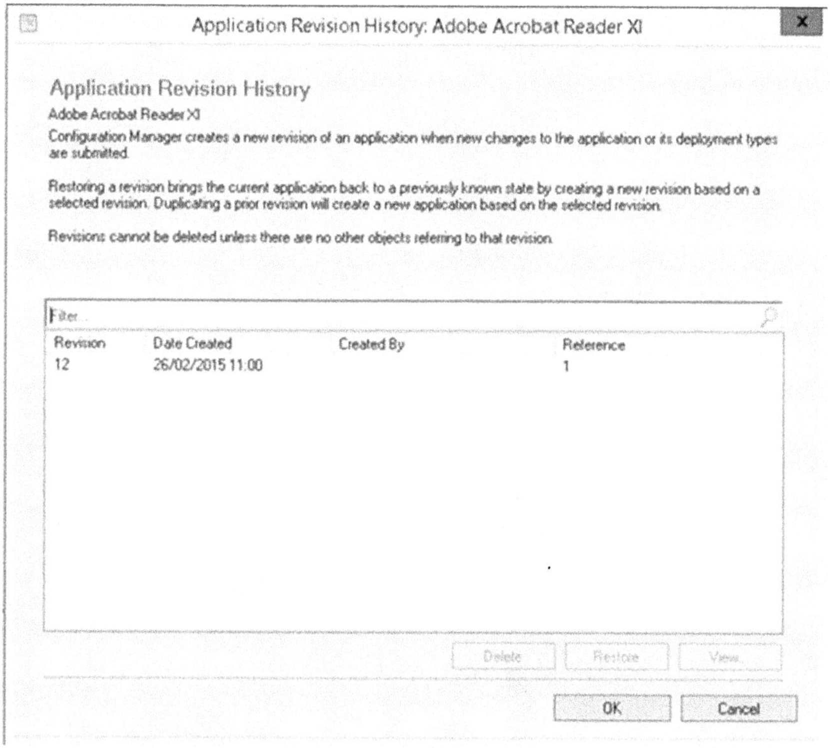

Figure 87. Part VII – Extras - Script 03 (1)

Script 04

Scenario: You are a consultant and you need to create an Automatic Deployment Rule (ADR) to test Windows Updates for Servers. This rule will run every time the Software Update Synchronizes with the Microsoft Update and will be deployed to a test collection.

Note: All command lines and scripts used can be found on the Part VI – Extras – Script 04.ps1 PowerShell script file

First, you need to set some variables to be used during the script; these variables will hold the following:

- The Configuration Manager Site Code
- The SMS Provider server name
- Automatic Deployment Rule Name
- Update Classifications
- Product List
- Language
- Collection Name and the Limiting Collection (in case you need to create the collection)
- The Deployment Package Name and Location

To achieve this, the script has the following lines:

```
$SiteCode = "CLC"
$SDKServer = "SRV0007"

$ADRName = "Windows Server Critical Updates"
$UpdateClassification = @("Critical Updates", "Security Updates")
$ProductList = @("Windows Server 2012 R2","Windows Server 2008 R2")
$Language = @("English")

$CollectionName = "Critical Updates"
$LimitCollection = "All Systems"

$PackageName = "PackageName"
$PackagePath = "\\Server\Share\ADRTest"
```

After this, you create a function called Create-CMDeploymentGroup, which creates a new Deployment Group or if one already exists, it will return the package ID. This is done by the Get-CMSoftwareUpdateDeploymentPackage. This is achieved by the following lines:

```
function Create-CMDeploymentGroup
{
    param (
        [string]$Name,
        [string]$sdkserver,
        [string]$SiteCode,
        [string]$Path
    )

    $DeploymentGroup = Get-CMSoftwareUpdateDeploymentPackage -Name
"$Name"

    if ($DeploymentGroup -eq $null)
    {
        $class = [wmiclass]""
        $class.psbase.path =
"\\$($sdkserver)\root\sms\site_$($sitecode):SMS_SoftwareUpdatesPackag
e"
        $DeploymentGroup = $class.CreateInstance()

        $DeploymentGroup.Name = $Name
        $DeploymentGroup.SourceSite = $SiteCode
        $DeploymentGroup.PkgSourcePath = "$($Path)\$($Name)"
        $DeploymentGroup.PkgSourceFlag = [int32]2

        $DeploymentGroup.put() | out-null
        $DeploymentGroup.Get() | out-null
    }

    return $DeploymentGroup.PackageID
}
```

The script actually starts here, you first import the Configuration Manager PowerShell module if it does not exist for the Site Code and after that, you move to the Configuration Manager site. This is achieved by the following lines:

```
import-module
$env:SMS_ADMIN_UI_PATH.Replace("bin\i386","bin\ConfigurationManager.p
sdl") -force

if ((get-psdrive $SiteCode -erroraction SilentlyContinue |
measure).Count -ne 1)
{
    new-psdrive -Name $SiteCode -PSProvider
"AdminUI.PS.Provider\CMSite" -Root $sdkserver
}
cd "$($SiteCode):"
```

The next part of the script will create, if needed, a collection and it is done by the Get-CMDeviceCollection and New-CMDeviceCollection cmdlets. This is achieved by the following lines:

```
$Coll = Get-CMDeviceCollection -Name "$CollectionName"
if ($Coll -eq $null)
{
    $Coll = New-CMDeviceCollection -Name "$CollectionName" -
LimitingCollectionName "$LimitCollection"
}
```

Once you have the collection, call the function Create-CMDeploymentGroup to create the Deployment Package if it is needed. This is achieved by the following lines:

```
Create-CMDeploymentGroup -Name"$PackageName" -sdkServer "$sdkserver"
-SiteCode "$SiteCode" -Path $PackagePath
```

Once you have the pre-requirements in place, create a new ADR, if needed using the Get-CMSoftwareUpdateAutoDeploymentRule and New-CMSoftwareUpdateAutoDeploymentRule cmdlets. This is achieved by the following lines:

```
$ADR = Get-CMSoftwareUpdateAutoDeploymentRule -Name "$ADRName"
if ($ADR -eq $null)
{
    $ADR = New-CMSoftwareUpdateAutoDeploymentRule -CollectionName
"$CollectionName" -DeploymentPackageName "$PackageName" -Name
"$ADRName" -AddToExistingSoftwareUpdateGroup $False -Superseded
$False -UpdateClassification $UpdateClassification -LanguageSelection
$Language -Product $ProductList
}
```

Lastly, you need to validate if the rule is enabled or not. Enable it, if it is not enabled. Check the property AutoDeploymentEnabled and if it is equal to $false, that means the rule is not enabled. You can enable the rule using the `Enable-CMSoftwareUpdateAutoDeploymentRule` cmdlet. This is achieved by the following lines:

```
if ($ADR.AutoDeploymentEnabled -eq $false)
{
    Enable-CMSoftwareUpdateAutoDeploymentRule -Name "$ADRName"
}
```

And as a result, you would see the Automatic Deployment Rule created

Figure 88. Part VII – Extras - Script 04 (1)

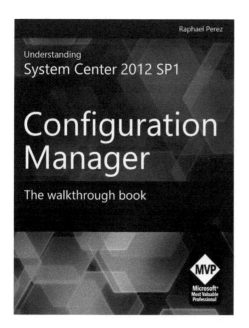

Understanding System Center 2012 SP1 Configuration Manager: The walkthrough book

A practical step-by-step guide to planning, installing, configuring and troubleshooting of System Center 2012 SP1 Configuration Manager

1. A step-by-step guide to managing your business devices

2. Discover how to have an up to date hardware and inventory

3. Discover how to manage Applications and Software Updates

4. Discover how to deploy a customized Operating System

www.ingramcontent.com/pod-product-compliance
Lightning Source LLC
Chambersburg PA
CBHW060144060326
40690CB00018B/3981